Strategic Investment and Finance

Ove Hedegaard & Michael Hedegaard

Strategic Investment and Finance

DJØF Publishing Copenhagen
2008

Strategic Investment
and Finance
First edition

DJØF Publishing is a company of the
Association of Danish Lawyers and Economists

Cover Design: Morten Højmark
Print: Narayana Press, Gylling
Binding: Damm's Forlagsbogbinderi, Randers

Printed in Denmark 2008
ISBN 978-87-574-1765-4

DJØF Publishing
17, Lyngbyvej
P.O.Box 2702
DK-2100 Copenhagen
Denmark

Phone: +45 39 13 55 00
Fax: +45 39 13 55 55
E-mail: forlag@djoef.dk
www.djoef-forlag.dk

CONTENTS

PREFACE

With Strategic Investment and Finanse our aim is to provide a comprehensive coverage of investment and finance theory applied in practice. A key focus has been to integrate business strategy into the topics and to present theories and models in ways that are concise and as easy to understand as possible.

Strategic investment and finance decisions are core to companies' long term success. We hope that this book creates value in this process by giving insights into the methodological as well as strategic elements in this important management area.

Traditional investment theory has concentrated on a mechanized estimation of cash flows and on minimising risks generally. But as the speed of change generally increases, then management needs to understand and adapt better to uncertainties. Flexibility and scenario thinking therefore becomes valuable tools. Strategic Investment and Finance provides a perspective along those lines by introducing real options and scenario analysis as useful models in this challenge.

The book's website http://www.djoef-forlag.dk/vare/8757417652 contains solutions to exercises and an investment model.

We would like to thank students, colleagues, friends and family who have contributed very much to this book. A special thanks goes to John Sanders. Without his involvement in this work, this book would not have been what it is today.

Copenhagen, June 2008

Ove Hedegaard Michael Hedegaard

CHAPTER 1

Introduction to Investment Theory

In this chapter we will first discuss the meaning of capital budgeting and investment analysis. Then we will classify investments into types and provide insights into the core elements of investment analysis.

In the business world, investments made are strategic decisions which should add value, improve the company's competitive position, and maximize shareholders value. Strategic investment and capital budgeting are critical to a corporation's success and form an integral part of strategic business planning and market positioning. This is because the analysis of investment opportunities impacts most of the strategic business decisions which companies undertake. Investments therefore encompass a wide variety of business decisions, from expansion of production capacity, to development of new technologies, entrance into new markets, mergers and acquisitions, investments in cost-saving equipment, and others. The distinguishing feature of investment decisions versus other company expenditures is that they involve costs and revenues seen over a number of years. This means that investment decisions typically involve large amounts of capital that, once made, are difficult to reverse. For this reason they attract the attention of management.

The focus of this book is on strategic corporate investment in capital asset projects, not financial investments in stocks and bonds. Unlike stocks and bonds, capital asset investment opportunities do not appear in a newspaper and are not touted on financial market talk-shows. They come from ideas and discussions within a company and must be turned reality. Strategic investments are therefore a combination of creativity, business strategy, and investment calculations. They require that a company be open to constantly exploring new ideas and making decisions about the opportunities which arise.

Investment projects can be classified in a number of ways as shown below:

- Replacement: Investments to replace obsolete equipment.
- Cost reduction: Investments to lower production costs by training employees, replacing old equipment, or relocating production facilities to areas where labor and raw materials are cheaper.
- Capacity expansion: Investments to meet increased demand for a company's products.
- New product introduction and market expansion: Investments to develop, produce, and sell new products and/or enter new markets.
- Government regulation: Investments made to comply with government requirements such as health and safety regulations, environmental standards, or other legal requirements.
- Welfare or social responsibility: Investments to improve employee welfare or address the social responsibility aspects of a company's operations.

As we see from this classification list, investments differ greatly in terms of risk and the amount of information available prior to committing funds. Naturally, there is a trade-off between comprehensive investment analysis and higher evaluation costs. If the decision is fairly routine, as in the case of replacing existing equipment, the investment may not warrant a lengthy analysis. However, risk increases when, for example, a company introduces new products or decides to enter new markets. Here, the need for comprehensive financial analysis and complete information is much greater. Of course, the size of the investment will also impact management's need for an in-depth investment analysis.

Another distinction between investment projects relates to their interaction with other company initiatives. They may be independent, mutually exclusive, or contingent. Independent investments can be accepted or rejected without regard to whether or not other investments are made. Mutually exclusive situations arise when one investment alternative excludes another, and vice-versa. This might happen when a firm must choose between two different suppliers of a new production line. Contingent investments, meanwhile, pose a situation where one investment is dependent upon a previous one being undertaken.

As we begin, we need to distinguish between investments and financing. *Investments* are a series of cash flows which begin with cash outflows and are followed by net inflows. *Financing* is just the opposite. It has cash inflows followed by net outflows, which typically take the form of installment payments.

The Objective of Strategic Investments

The purpose of investing is to add value to a company in a way that achieves its goals and increases shareholder wealth. This concept implies that investments must be evaluated based on their ability to generate positive future cash flows. However, as we will discuss in detail in Chapter 7, this is not as clear-cut as it may seem. Future cash flows can be difficult to estimate on their own, but a company's overall objectives will be influenced by the demands of its various stakeholders.

The stakeholder model in Figure 1.1 shows some of the most important stakeholder groups in a typical company. These groups may have differing objectives, thereby clouding the company's overall goal structure and making it more complex.

The criteria which each stakeholder uses to evaluate an investment may vary. So, too, may the weight which the investment's financial criteria will carry. This book will focus on creating shareholder value but also consider many issues from the stakeholders' perspective.

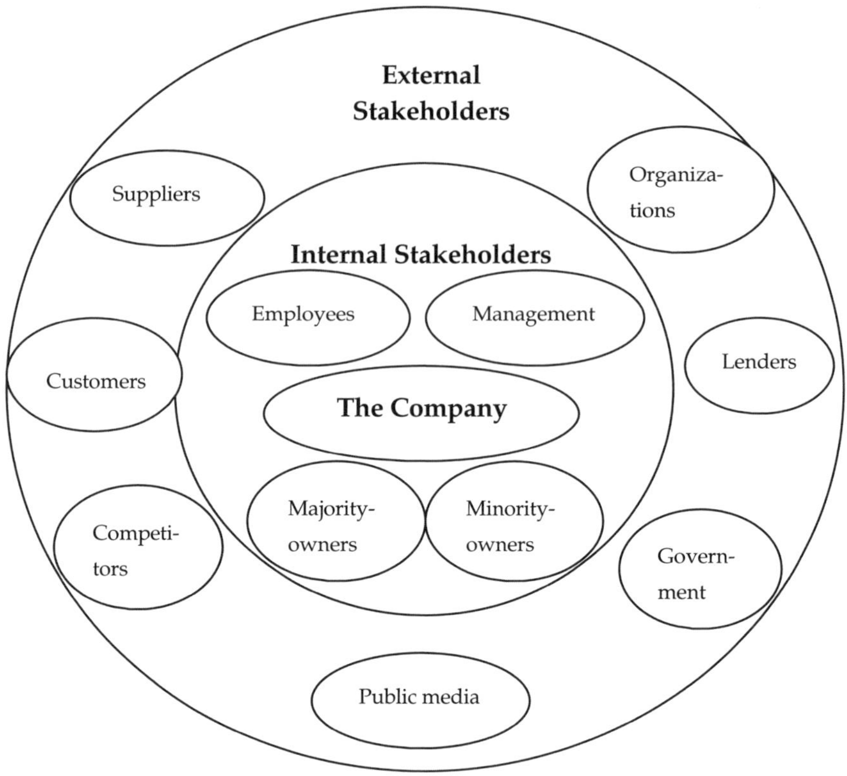

Figure 1.1 The stakeholder model

Investment Analysis

Shareholder value is increased when an investment's expected future cash flows exceed the initial outflow after being discounted back to the present. This is where we will focus, namely on the incremental cash flows derived from the investment decision. Investment analysis therefore involves estimating of future cash flows over time and then discounting them back to the investment's starting point. This raises two fundamental issues which we will discuss below: 1) how to spread the cash flows properly over time, and 2) how to make these cash flows comparable to each other. The first issue has to do with timing of cash flows, the second with the discount interest rate that is used.

An excellent way to visualize expected future cash flows is to plot them on a time-axis. By convention, cash inflows are drawn as upward-pointing arrows at their time of occurrence on the time-axis and cash outflows are naturally drawn downwards. The size or amount of cash inflow or outflow determines the length of the arrow, as illustrated below:

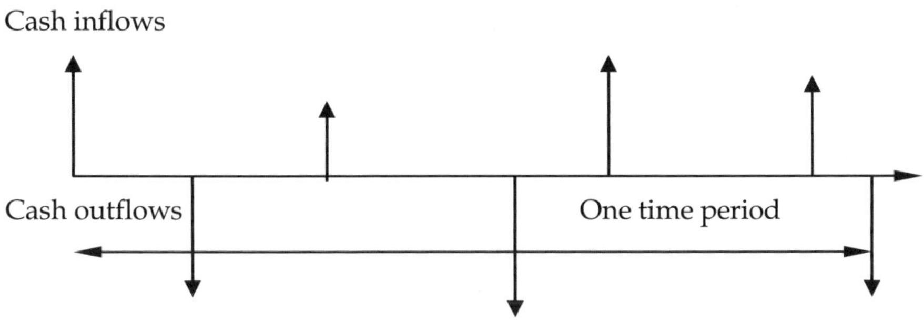

Figure 1.2 Several cash inflows and cash outflows occurring in the same time period

Instead of plotting many cash inflows and outflows at different moments of the same time period, we can combine them into a net total and place them at the end of the single period's time-axis. This is shown in Figure 1.3 below:

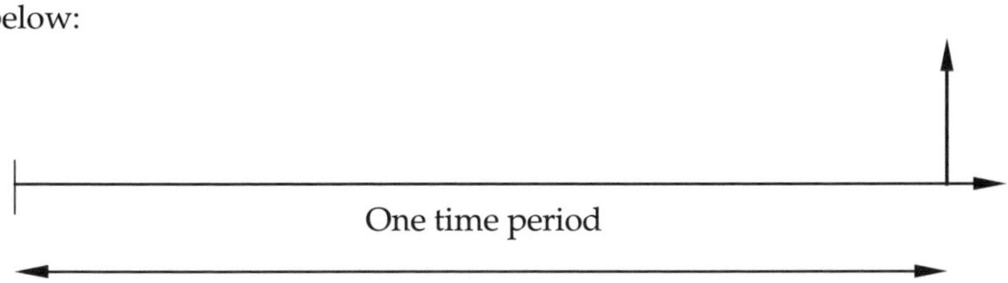

Figure 1.3 The single time period's net cash flow

The conventions we will use are as follows:

- All cash inflows and cash outflows within the same time period are assumed to occur at its conclusion.
- Cash outflows are netted against cash inflows occurring within the same time period. This is done without regard to

whether they take place at different moments in the time period because as long as they fall within it, they are able to offset one another.

Within each time period that we define for our investment analysis, we therefore calculate a net cash flow, which is the sum of all cash inflows minus all cash outflows. This resulting net cash flow is assumed to take place at the end of the given time period. This convention facilitates investment analysis and helps to keep things simple.

The length of the time period used by an investor or investment analyst depends on personal preference and/or the situation at hand, this could be yearly, semi-annually, quarterly or even monthly. The most important consideration is that the time lapse between same-period cash flows be seen as unimportant by the investor. When this is true, the cash inflows and outflows from Figure 1.2 can be summed into one net cash flow and plotted at the end of the time period as shown in Figure 1.3. Because the overall time period is short enough, the investor is indifferent as to whether the actual cash flow stream is represented by Figure 1.2 or Figure 1.3.

Discounting

Once we have defined our time period and estimated the net cash flow at the end of each one, spreading them out over time, we need to make them comparable. For this we use discounting. Discounting is the process where we take all of our future net cash flows and translate them back to the present time. The principle is similar to looking at the windmills on the book cover: Windmills (and cash flows) which occur further out appear smaller than those which are close at hand. In order to make them comparable we use discounting, where we must first select a discount rate to get the perspective right.

The discount rate, or cost of capital, is a reflection of:

- *Positive time preference.* An investment will typically involve foregoing the current consumption of goods in exchange for consumption in the future. Yet because consumption today is preferred to consumption later, a measure of compensation will be needed. This utility is reflected in the discount rate.

- *Risk.* Investing in the future entails a certain degree of risk. The discount rate therefore includes a risk premium which depends on the amount of investment risk.
- *Inflation.* Investors require that the amount of funds invested maintain its purchasing power. If cash flows are adjusted for the expected rate of inflation, the discount rate must also be adjusted by this amount.
- *Taxes.* Taxes must be paid out of an investment's cash flow and are therefore similar to inflation. Cash flows that are adjusted for tax payments should incorporate a discount rate which reflects the amount of tax.

We see from these points above that the discount rate is equal to the cost of capital, which is defined as the price of using money for the opportunity at hand. Its value is largely subjective because each investor places a different value on the time preference for spending money now rather than later.

The risk element is somewhat more complicated. Theoretically this element compensates an investor for the *perceived* risk of the investment project in question. However, a given project can be perceived by well-informed investors as having a lower risk profile than that which investors with lesser knowledge of the critical risk elements would give it. If a company's stakeholders associate different degrees of risk with a given investment project, it becomes even more complicated to agree on the risk premium required.

Adjustment for inflation and tax are more straightforward. If an investment's cash flows are subject to these factors, the discount rate should be adjusted as well. This topic is covered in depth in Chapter 6.

Applying the above definitions properly can be difficult in practice. However, since we know that the discount rate is equal to the cost of capital we can analyze the project's cost of capital and simplify things greatly. Assuming that the project is financed by debt and equity, there are two elements in the cost of capital:

1. The cost of debt
2. The cost of equity (opportunity cost)

With the cost of capital method, we look at the costs required to source the investment's capital. Debt financing is fairly straightforward to price because interest rates can be observed and negotiated in the market. Chapter 10 will discuss the pricing of debt in detail.

The cost of equity, or *opportunity cost,* reflects the fact that a company's shareholders forego the possibility of gains on an alternative investment with the same risk profile if they choose to invest in the project at hand.

After calculating the price of each element in cost of capital, we can combine them into the Weighted Average Cost of Capital, or WACC:

$$WACC = w_e \cdot k_e + w_d \cdot k_d$$

where,

w_e is the proportion of equity capital in the total capital structure
k_e is the cost of equity.
w_d is the proportion of debt capital in the total capital structure
K_d is the cost of debt.

Example 1.1
An investment project costing €1 million (total capital structure) will be financed by €0.6 million in debt and €0.4 million in equity. Debt financing has an interest rate (cost of debt) of 8 % p.a., and the required rate of return investors require (cost of equity) is 15 % p.a.:

$$WACC = € 0.6/(€ 0.6+€ 0.4) \cdot 8\ \% + € 0.4/(€ 0.6+€ 0.4) \cdot 15\ \% = 10.8\ \%\ p.a.$$

Evaluating Investments

Once we understand how to structure expected future cash flows and have a discount rate which makes cash flows comparable over time, there are four classical methods we can use to evaluate investment strategies:

1. *Net Present Value, or NPV*. This measure of profitability expresses an investment's degree of value creation. Net Present Value takes all of an investment's future cash flows and discounts them back to Time 0, then adds them together. Therefore a positive NPV represents value creation, whereas a negative NPV is equivalent to value reduction.

2. *Annuity Value*. Having calculated an investment's NPV we can convert it into equal annual cash flows spread out over the number of time periods used in the analysis. The annuity provides the average yield of the investment over its life span. An investment with a positive average yield should be accepted, whereas one with a negative average yield should be rejected.

3. *Internal Rate of Return, or IRR*. The IRR calculates the rate of return on an investment which corresponds to an NPV of 0. The IRR therefore measures the average gain which the invested money generates in each time period. If the internal rate of return is greater than the cost of capital, then the investment is profitable.

4. *Payback Period*. This calculates the number of periods required for the investment's cumulative expected cash flow to equal the initial investment. If the calculated payback period is shorter than that required by investors, then the investment should be made.

CHAPTER 2

Discounting

Discounting is a finance tool which is used to make cash flows generated at different points in time comparable to one another. We therefore need a discounting rate which reflects the cost of capital. The *cost of capital* is defined as the price incurred in each time period for committing finances to a given project.

For example, if we were to borrow all the money needed for a project, the cost of capital for €1 would be the interest rate we pay. It is normally referred to as *I*. I = 0.05 means that it costs €0.05 to hold €1 for one time period. It implies that the borrower has a choice of paying €1 now or waiting one time period and paying €1 + I. Often, the cost of capital is expressed as a percent, and an interest rate of 0.05 is equivalent to 5 % per time period and can also be written as 5 % p.a.

The length of a time period may vary from case to case but will typically be a year, six months, a quarter, or a month. There is no fixed rule for a period's duration and in principle it can be any length of time. For bank loans and deposits a time period is usually defined as the time interval between two consecutive interest calculations. Credit cards from finance companies and shopping mall vendors typically accumulate interest each month, whereas banks and credit institutions usually calculate interest on a quarterly or semi-annual basis.

In discounting, it makes no difference whether you apply the creditor's (also called investor's) point of view or the debtor's. The amount the debtor pays in interest is the same amount which the creditor receives.

Simple Discounting

With simple discounting you calculate how much money an amount grows by per time period. If you borrow €1 at interest rate *I* you must repay €1 + I after one time period. The following terms are fundamental to understanding this relationship:

NPV_0	Net Present Value is the size of the amount borrowed today.
FV_1	Future Value is the amount borrowed plus the interest I that must be repaid after one time period.

The relationship between NPV_0 and FV_1 can be expressed as follows:

$$FV_1 = NPV_0 \cdot (1 + I).$$

This means that NPV_0 grows by a factor of 1 plus the interest rate I throughout one time period. This can be illustrated graphically as shown in Figure 2.1:

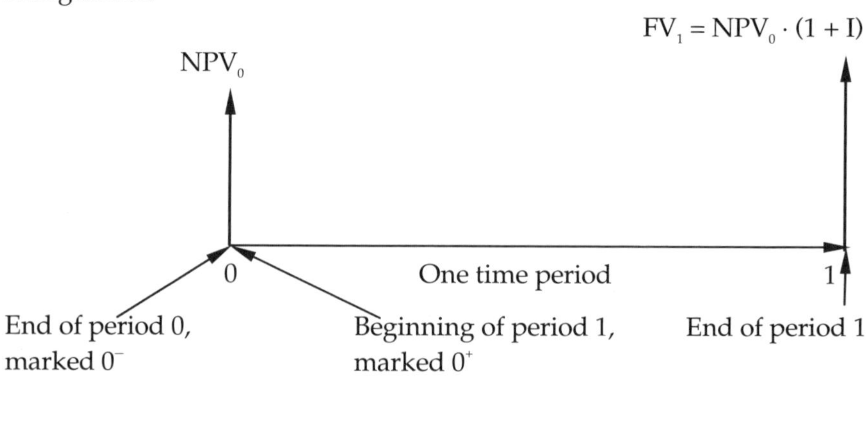

Figure 2.1 Calculation of interest and future value for 1 time period

Said another way, the future value at Time 1 for an amount NPV_0 at Time 0 is expressed as: $NPV_0 \cdot (1 + I)$.

The two amounts, NPV_0 and FV_1, are assumed to have the same value for both debtor and creditor because the difference in time is offset by the difference in the size of the amount. Therefore, the two parties are indifferent as to whether they receive NPV_0 now or FV_1 after one time period.

Of the three numbers, NPV_0, FV_1, and interest rate *I*, if you know any two of them, you can deduce the third from the relationship between them:

$$FV_1 = NPV_0 \cdot (1+I) \tag{2.1}$$

$$NPV_0 = \frac{FV_1}{(1+I)} = FV_1 \cdot (1+I)^{-1} \tag{2.2}$$

$$1+I = \frac{FV_1}{NPV_0} \Rightarrow I = \frac{FV_1}{NPV_0} - 1 \tag{2.3}$$

Consequently, if you wish to know how much money you should set aside today at a given interest rate in order to withdraw a certain amount one time period from now, you can use Formula (2.2), where FV_1 and the interest rate I are known and NPV_0 is calculated.

If you know how much money is borrowed or lent today and how much it will be worth in one time period, you can use Formula (2.3) to calculate the implied interest rate.

Example 2.1
You deposit €100,000 at a 10 % p.a. interest rate. How much will you have in your account after one year?

$FV_1 = NPV_0 \cdot (1 + I).$
$FV_1 = €100{,}000 \cdot (1 + 0.10) = €110{,}000.$

Example 2.2
An account that yields an interest rate of 8 % per year must have a balance of €5,000 after 1 year. How much would you need to deposit now?

$NPV_0 = FV_1 \cdot (1 + I)^{-1}.$
$NPV_0 = 5{,}000 \cdot (1 + 0.08)^{-1} = €4{,}629.63.$

Example 2.3
By depositing €2,000 in an account, you will be able to withdraw € 2,140 after 1 year. What is the interest rate?

$$I = \frac{FV_1}{NPV_0} - 1.$$

$$I = \frac{2{,}140}{2{,}000} - 1 = 0.07 \text{ or } 7\ \% \text{ p.a.}$$

Compounded Interest

Discounting one amount back and forth in time
Usually, discounted cash flows run for more than one time period. If NPV_0 indicates the amount provided at Time 0, it will have grown to the following amount in one time period:

$$FV_1 = NPV_0 \cdot (1 + I).$$

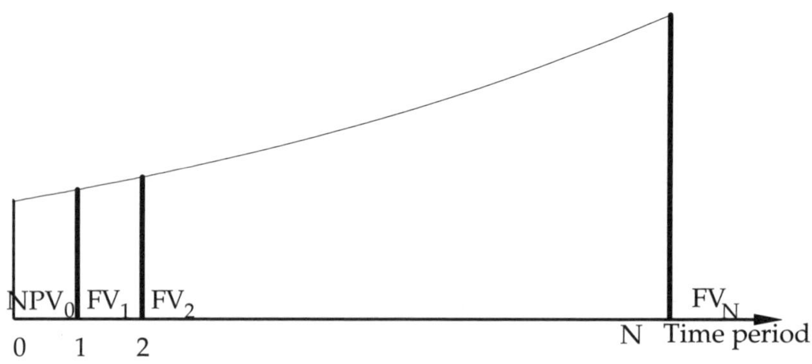

Figure 2.2 Interest calculations for more than one time period

If the payment is postponed until a second time period, the available amount will be:

$$FV_2 = FV_1 \cdot (1 + I).$$

For every additional time period the amount is compounded, you multiply by (1 + I). That is:

$$
\begin{aligned}
&FV_1 = NPV_0 \cdot (1 + I). \\
&FV_2 = NPV_0 \cdot (1 + I) \cdot (1 + I) = && NPV_0 \cdot (1 + I)^2. \\
&FV_3 = NPV_0 \cdot (1 + I) \cdot (1 + I) \cdot (1 + I) = && NPV_0 \cdot (1 + I)^3. \\
&\ldots \\
&\ldots \\
&FV_N = && NPV_0 \cdot (1 + I)^N.
\end{aligned}
$$

The value of the cash flow, accumulated over N periods of time, is found by multiplying the initial amount of money by $(1 + I)^N$:

$$FV_N = NPV_0 \cdot (1 + I)^N. \tag{2.4}$$

This means that $NPV_0 \cdot (1 + I)^N$ after N periods has the same value as NPV_0 today. This formula is called the *compound interest formula* and $(1+I)^N$ is called the *future value interest factor, $FVIF_{I,N}$*. It is fundamental to understanding investment theory and it enables us to compare cash flows that occur at different points in time.

We can now introduce four new formulas to explain the relationship between NPV_0, FV_N, the interest rate *I*, and the number of time periods N. With these formulas, if you know any three of the relevant values you can always calculate the fourth:

$$FV_N = NPV_0 \cdot (1+I)^N \tag{2.4}$$

$$NPV_0 = \frac{FV_N}{(1+I)^N} = FV_N \cdot (1+I)^{-N} \tag{2.5}$$

$$(1+I)^N = \frac{FV_N}{NPV_0} \Rightarrow (1+I) = \sqrt[N]{\frac{FV_N}{NPV_0}} \Rightarrow I = \sqrt[N]{\frac{FV_N}{NPV_0}} - 1 \tag{2.6}$$

If the number of time periods N is unknown but NPV_0, FV_N and the interest *I* are known, you can calculate N by using the following formula:

$$(1+I)^N = \frac{FV_N}{NPV_0}.$$

This is done by trial and error or by taking the log on both sides of the equation:

$$N \cdot ln(1+R) = ln\,NPV_N - ln\,NPV_0 \Rightarrow N = \frac{ln\,NPV_N - ln\,NPV_0}{ln(1+R)} \quad (2.7)$$

These seven formulas, of which the last six can be traced back to Formula (2.1), are the core of discounting.

Remember: $(1+I)^N > (1+I) > 1$.

Amounts grow when compounded into the future and can be discounted back to the present.

The factor $(1 + I)^{-N}$ is called the *present value interest factor* or *discounting facto*, $PVIF_{I,N}$.

Remember: $(1+I)^{-N} < (1+I)^{-1} < 1$.

Amounts decrease when discounted back in time.

Example 2.4
You deposit €7,000 in an account that yields an interest of 5 % per year. How much is available on the account after 7 years?

$FV_N = NPV_0 \cdot (1 + I)^N$.
$FV_7 = 7{,}000 \cdot (1 + 0.05)^7$.

Using either a financial calculator or a spread sheet we can now determine FV_7:

$FV_7 = 7{,}000 \cdot 1.40710 =$ €9,849.70.

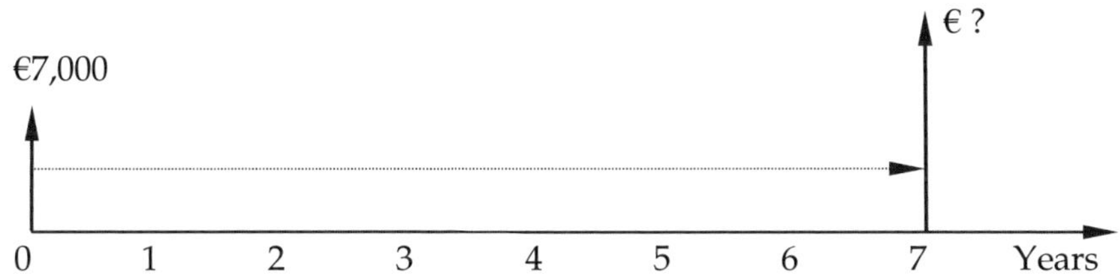

An amount of €7,000 deposited at 5 % interest per year will grow to €9,849.70 in 7 years.

Example 2.5
A creditor demands an interest rate of 1.5 % per month to lend €10,000 today. How much is to be repaid in 8 months to liquidate the loan?

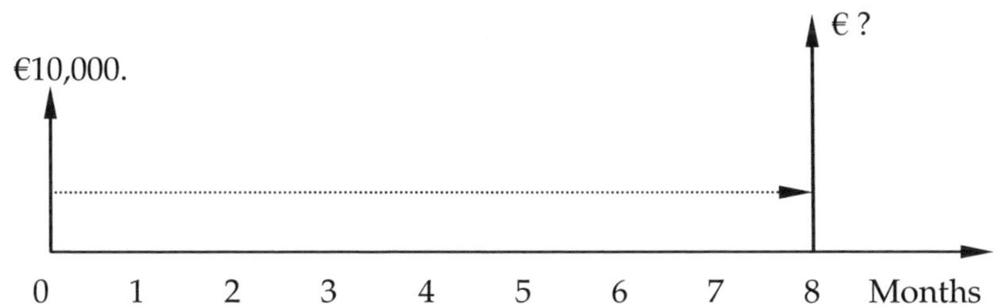

$$FV_N = NPV_0 \cdot (1 + R)^N.$$
$$FV_8 = 10{,}000 \cdot (1 + 0.015)^8.$$
$$FV_8 = 10{,}000 \cdot 1.12649 = €11{,}264.90.$$

Thus, €10,000 of debt at an interest rate of 1.5 % per month will grow to €11,264.90 in 8 months.

Example 2.6
An account that yields an interest rate of 8 % per year should have a balance of €10,000 after 7 years. How much would you need to deposit today in order to realize this goal?

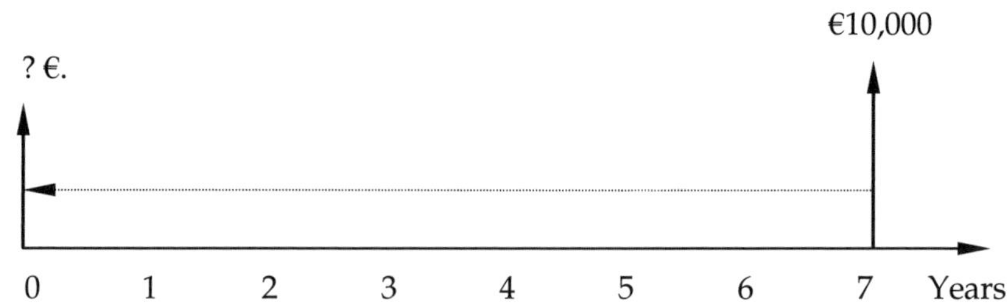

$$NPV_0 = FV_N \cdot (1 + I)^{-N}.$$
$$NPV_0 = 10{,}000 \cdot (1+0.08)^{-7} = €5{,}834.90.$$

Example 2.7

€4,000 will grow to €8,000 in 8 years. What is the corresponding annual rate of interest?

$$\boldsymbol{I} = \sqrt[N]{\frac{\boldsymbol{FV_N}}{\boldsymbol{NPV_0}}} - 1.$$

$$\boldsymbol{I} = \sqrt[8]{\frac{8{,}000}{4{,}000}} - 1 = 0.0905 \text{ or } 9.05\ \% \text{ p.a.}$$

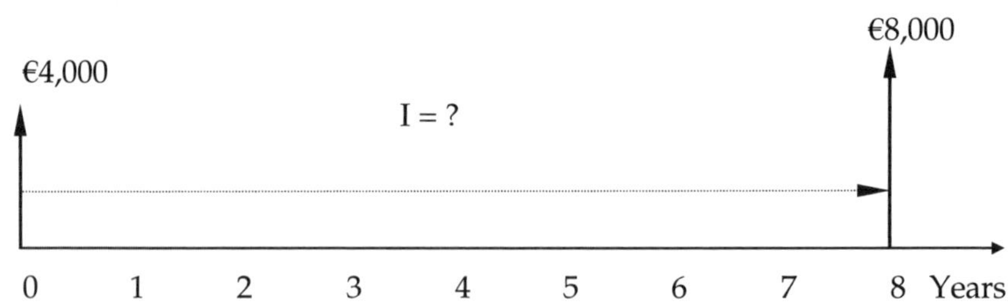

Example 2.8

How many years will it take for €7,000 yielding 7 % per year to grow to €13,770?

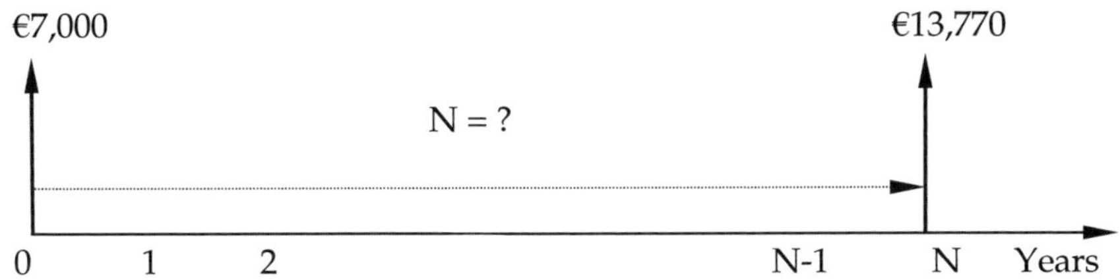

$$N = \frac{\ln FV_N - \ln NPV_0}{\ln(1+I)}.$$

$$N = \frac{9.53025 - 8.85367}{0.06766} = 10 \text{ years}.$$

Example 2.9
14 years from now, you would like to have €15,000 in your bank account. If the deposit yields an interest rate of 4 % per year, how much must you deposit today in order to achieve your plan?

$NPV_0 = FV_N \cdot (1 + I)^{-N}$.
$NPV_0 = 15{,}000 \cdot (1 + 0.04)^{-14}$.
Using spread sheet or a financial calculator NPV_0 is determined to be:

$NPV_0 = 15{,}000 \cdot 0.577475 = €\ 8{,}662.13$.

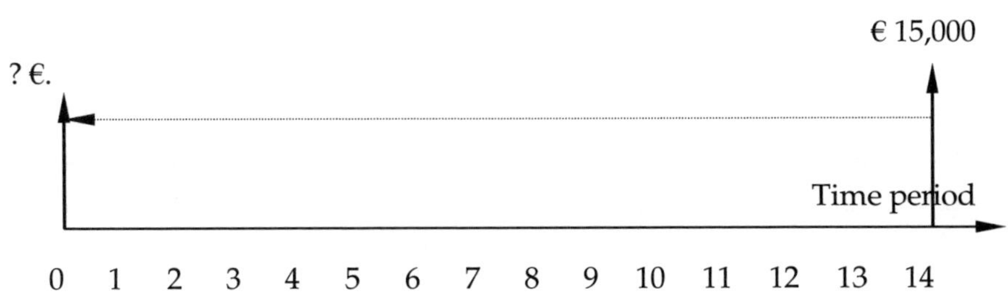

You will need to deposit € 8,662.13 today at a fixed interest rate of 4 % in order to have €15,000 in your account after 14 years.

Discounting different amounts forth and back in time
To borrow or invest is a strategic long-term decision that will typically result in a number of cash inflows and outflows staggered over a period of

time. Therefore we need tools to evaluate future cash flows in relation to a present value. For this, we use the rules from simple and compounded discounting where all individual cash flows can be discounted either:

- Back and forth in time.
- Back to Time 0, or
- to a randomly chosen reference time.

By discounting different cash flows to the same given point in time we can make them comparable. To determine the total future value of a number of cash flows at *N* point in time, you need to translate every cash flow to that point in time using the compound interest formula. We define the net cash flow at Time *t* as CF_t. Also, we regard this net cash flow as the sum of all cash inflows minus all cash outflows within the time period. The sequence of future cash flows is given as:

$$FV_N = CF_0 \cdot (1+I)^N + CF_1 \cdot (1+I)^{N-1} + CF_2 \cdot (1+I)^{N-2} + \cdots + CF_{N-1} \cdot (1+I) + CF_N.$$

This can be written more concisely as:

$$FV_N = \sum_{t=0}^{N} CF_t \cdot (1+I)^{N-t} \tag{2.8}$$

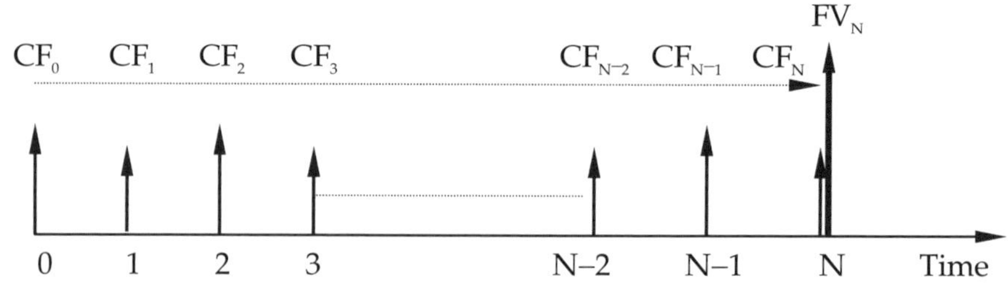

Figure 2.3 Future value of a number of different cash flows

Example 2.10

A young woman deposits and withdraws the following amounts at the given points in time:

Time t	Amount
0	€3,000
1	€4,000
3	– €2,000
5	€7,000

How much will be available on her account at Point 8 in time if the deposit yields an interest rate of 3.5 % per time period? (Notice that at Point 3 in time, €2,000 is withdrawn)

In order to calculate the total amount, you need to translate the four cash flows forward in time to Point 8, then add them together. The easiest way to do this is by drawing a table where the column FV_8 represents the individual amounts discounted forward to Point 8 in time.

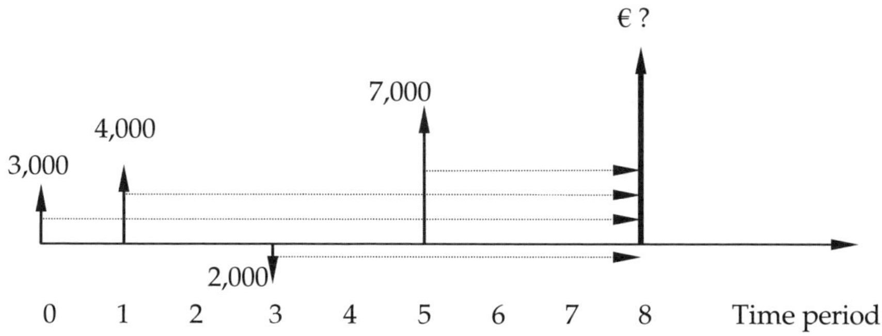

Time t	Amount	$(1 + R)^{8-t}$	FV_8
0	3,000	1.316809	€3,950.43
1	4,000	1.272279	€5,089.12
3	–2,000	1.187686	€–2,375.37
5	7,000	1.108718	€7,761.03
8		**Total**	**€14,425.20**

The total deposit at Point 8 in time will be €14,425.20.

Example 2.11
A student who cannot get by on his scholarship and part-time work takes the following loans at a rate of 4 % interest per year:

Time t	Amount
0	€1,500
1	€2,000
2	€1,200
3	€2,500
4	€3,000

How large is the total amount borrowed by Year 4 immediately after the final loan is received?

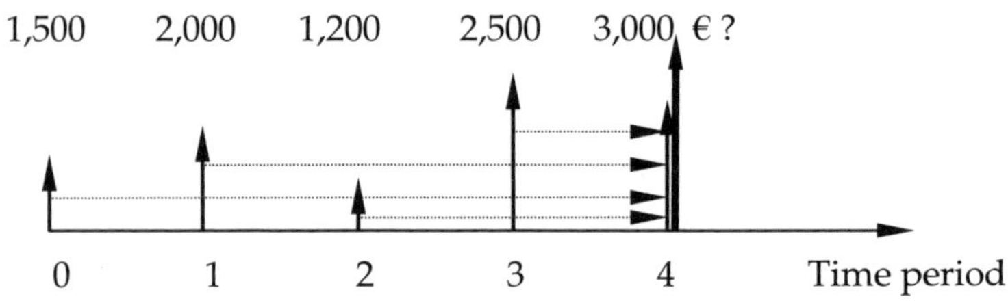

The student's total debt can be determined by drawing a table with the necessary information and calculations. If you use a financial calculator or a spreadsheet it is sufficient to type in the years, amounts, and interest rate per year to calculate the total amount owed.

Year t	Amount	No. of years, (4 – t)	$(1 + I)^{4-t}$	FV_4
0	€1,500	4	1.169859	€1,754.79
1	€2,000	3	1.124864	€2,249.73
2	€1,200	2	1.0816	€1,297.92
3	€2,500	1	1.04	€2,600.00
4	€3,000	0	1	€3,000.00
			Total	**€10,902.44**

The student's total debt immediately after raising the last part of the loan will be €10,902.44

In the same way that a number of individual cash flows can be compounded forward to the end point in time and summed, each individual amount can be discounted back to Time 0 and added there.

$$NPV_0 = CF_0 + CF_1 \cdot (1 + I)^{-1} + CF_2 \cdot (1 + I)^{-2} + \cdots + CF_N \cdot (1 + I)^{-N}.$$

This can also be written as:

$$\boldsymbol{NPV_0} = \sum_{t=0}^{N} \boldsymbol{CF_t} \cdot (1+\boldsymbol{I})^{-t} \qquad (2.9)$$

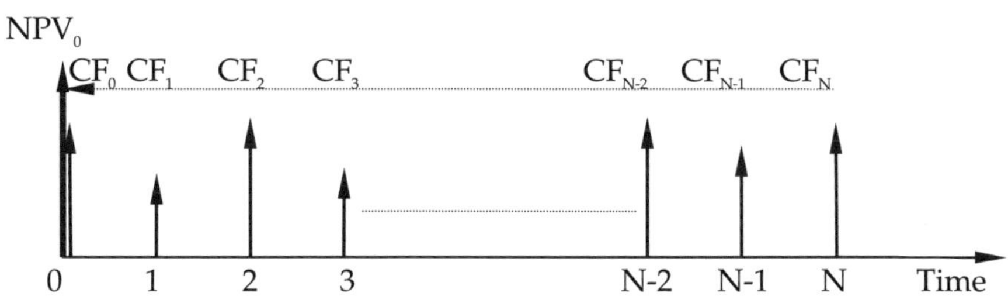

Figure 2.4 Net present value of different amounts

Example 2.12

A provident man is about to retire and wishes to cushion the transition from working life. He would like to do this by depositing money into a bank account and using the funds to supplement his pension. Over the first five years of retirement, the man wishes to withdraw the following sums from the account:

Year t	Amount
1	€100,000
2	€80,000
3	€60,000
4	€40,000
5	€20,000

How much money must he deposit in the account at the commencement of retirement if it is assumed that:

- The first withdrawal from the account will take place one year after retirement
- The deposit will yield an interest of 4.5 % p.a.?

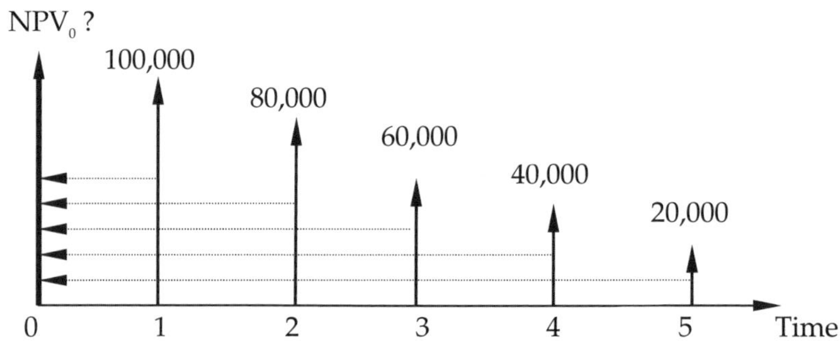

Time t	Amount	$(1 + I)^{-t}$	NPV_0	Total NPV_0
0				**€271,121.45**
1	€100,000	0.956938	€95,693.78	
2	€80,000	0.915730	€73,258.40	
3	€60,000	0.876297	€52,577.80	
4	€40,000	0.838561	€33,542.45	
5	€20,000	0.802451	€16,049.02	

In order to ensure a smooth transition, the man should deposit €271,121.45 at the commencement of retirement.

Annuities

In many cases a cash flow consists of a number of equal amounts payable at fixed time intervals. This type of cash flow is called an *annuity*. These circumstances often apply to the repayment of loans, various savings plans with a fixed payment occurring at predetermined times, most installment purchases and lease contracts, etc. In these cases the formulas for discounting cash flows back and forth in time can be simplified significantly:

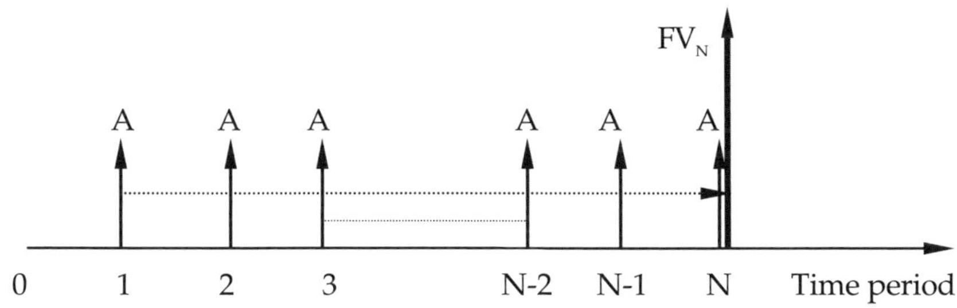

Figure 2.5 Future value of an annuity

If you use formula (2.8) it holds that:

$$FV_N = \sum_{t=1}^{N} CF_t \cdot (1+I)^{N-t}.$$

Since CF_t is the same in all time periods and is equal to A, we see that:

$$FV_N = \sum_{t=1}^{N} A \cdot (1+I)^{N-t}.$$

Putting A outside the summation sign, the expression for FV_N can be written as:

$$FV_N = A \cdot \sum_{t=1}^{N} (1+I)^{N-t}.$$

The expression $\sum_{t=1}^{N} (1+I)^{N-t}$ is the sum of (1 + I) over N-t time periods. Therefore, FV_N can be written as:

$$FV_N = A \cdot \frac{(1+I)^N - 1}{I}. \qquad (2.10a)$$

The factor $\frac{(1+I)^N - 1}{I}$ is called the *future value interest factor for an annuity* and is written as $FVIFA_{I,N}$. The annuity compound factor gives the future value of equal payments of €1 per time period, over N time periods.

$$FV_N = A \cdot FVIFA_{I,N} \qquad (2.10b)$$

Remember: $FVIFA_{I,N} > 1.$

By solving for A in the formula (2.10b), we get:

$$A = \frac{FV_N}{FVIFA_{I,N}} = FV_N \cdot \frac{1}{FVIFA_{I,N}}. \qquad (2.11)$$

Remember: $\frac{1}{FVIFA_{I,N}} < 1.$

Formula (2.11) can be used to determine how much money must be paid at fixed time intervals in order to reach a certain total by the end of the overall period.

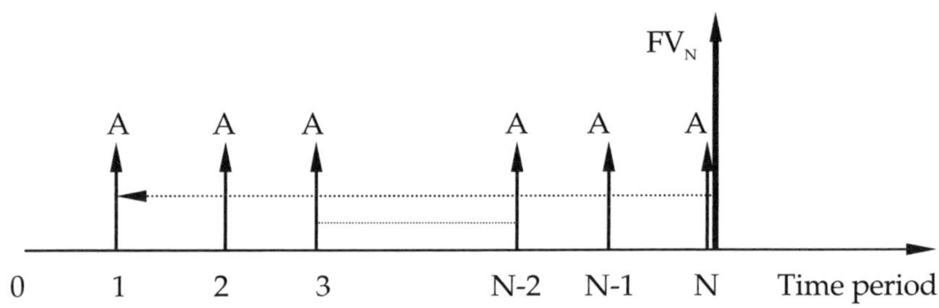

Figure 2.6 Future value split into an annuity

Whether the future value of an annuity or its net present value should be calculated depends on the situation at hand. With installment purchases or loan agreements, we can calculate the net present value of a number of equal future payments.

Applying the same discounting principle used previously to a number of equal payments forward in time, we can calculate the net present value of an annuity by using Formula (2.9):

$$NPV_0 = \sum_{t=0}^{N} CF_t \cdot (1+I)^{-t} = \sum_{t=1}^{N} A \cdot (1+I)^{-t} = A \sum_{t=1}^{N} (1+I)^{-t}.$$

After rewriting, we are left with:

$$NPV_0 = A \cdot \frac{(1+I)^N - 1}{(1+I)^N \cdot I}. \qquad (2.12a)$$

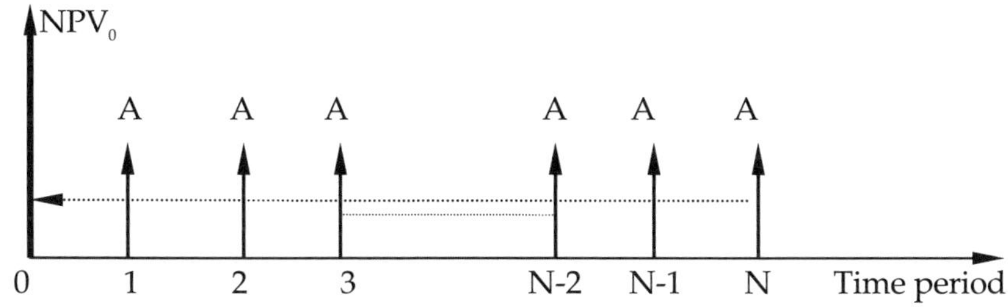

Figure 2.7 Present value of an annuity

The factor $\frac{(1+I)^N - 1}{(1+I)^N \cdot I}$ is called *the present value interest factor for an annuity ($PVIFA_{I,N}$)*. The factor calculates the present value of a payment of €1 per time period for N time periods.

$$NPV_0 = A \cdot PVIFA_{I,N} \qquad (2.12b)$$

Remember: $PVIFA_{I,N} > 1$ *if* $N \geq 2$ *and* $I < 60\ \%$ *per time period.*

If N is a perpetuity we see that:

$$NPV_0 = A \cdot \frac{1}{I}. \qquad (2.12c)$$

Isolating A in Formula (2.12b) gives:

$$A = \frac{NPV_0}{PVIFA_{I,N}} = NPV_0 \cdot PVIFA_{I,N}^{-1}. \qquad (2.13)$$

The factor $PVIFA_{I,N}^{-1}$ is called the *annuity factor*. The factor indicates how much must be paid per time period over N time periods to cover the interest and repayment of €1.

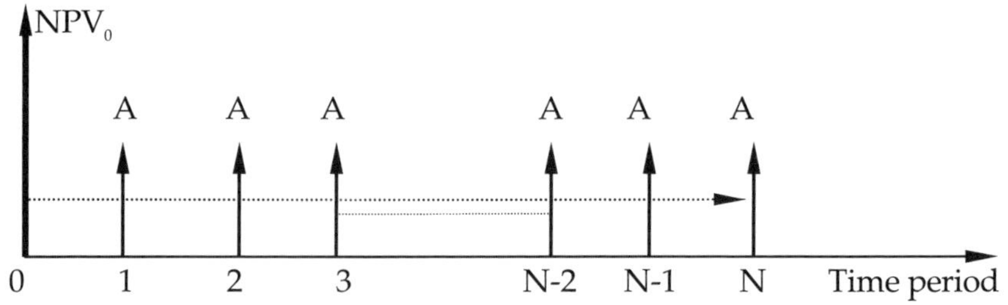

Figure 2.8 Dividing net present value into an annuity

NPV_0 is discounted to Time 0, which is the beginning of the first time period.

Unless explicitly stated otherwise, an annuity's net present value is calculated at the beginning of the first time period (Time 0). Also, its first payment always takes place at the end of the first time period (Time 1). Meanwhile, FV_N is calculated at the end of time period N, immediately after the last payment.

Example 2.13
A young couple would like to save in order to buy a house. They decide to deposit €2,000 in a savings account in December each year. The account yields an interest rate of 6 % p.a. which is calculated once a year. How much will the young couple have for the down payment immediately after they have made the seventh deposit?

$FV_N = A \cdot FVIFA_{I,N}.$
$FV_7 = 2{,}000 \cdot FVIFA_{6\%,7}.$
$FV_7 = 2{,}000 \cdot 8.39384 = €16{,}787.68.$

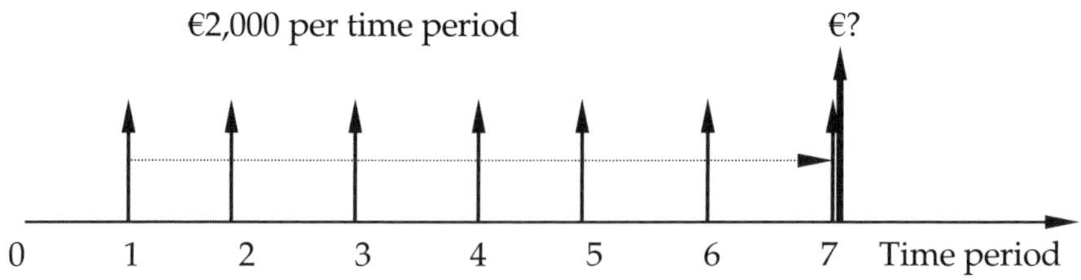

If the savings plan is followed precisely, the couple will have €16,787.68 available for a down payment after making the seventh deposit.

Example 2.14

A certain item may be purchased either outright or on an instalment plan. If the instalment plan is used there will be no down payment, but €10,000 must be paid at the end of every year for six years. If the interest rate is 10 % per year, what is the item's selling price if purchased outright today?

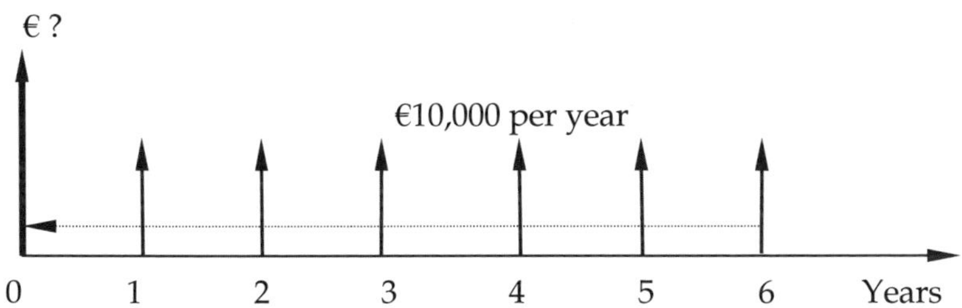

$$NPV_0 = A \cdot PVIFA_{I,N}.$$
$$NPV_0 = 10{,}000 \cdot PVIFA_{10\%,6}.$$
$$NPV_0 = 10{,}000 \cdot 4.35526 \quad = €43{,}552.60.$$

Example 2.15

A couple wants to save €150,000 within 8 years. How much will they need to deposit each year if their savings account pays 5 % interest per year?

$$\boldsymbol{A = FV_N \cdot FVIFA_{I,N}^{-1}}.$$
$$A = 150{,}000 \cdot \boldsymbol{FVIFA_{5\%,8}^{-1}}.$$
$$A = 150{,}000 \cdot 0.104722 \quad = €15{,}708.30.$$

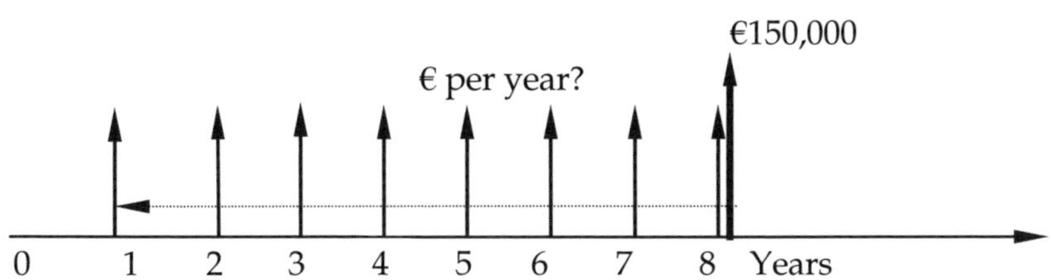

With an annual interest rate of 5 %, the couple would need to deposit €15,708.30 per year for 8 years in order to save €150,000.

Example 2.16

A loan of €150,000 must be paid off over 8 years with equal payments each year. What is the annual payment if the interest rate is 5 % per year?

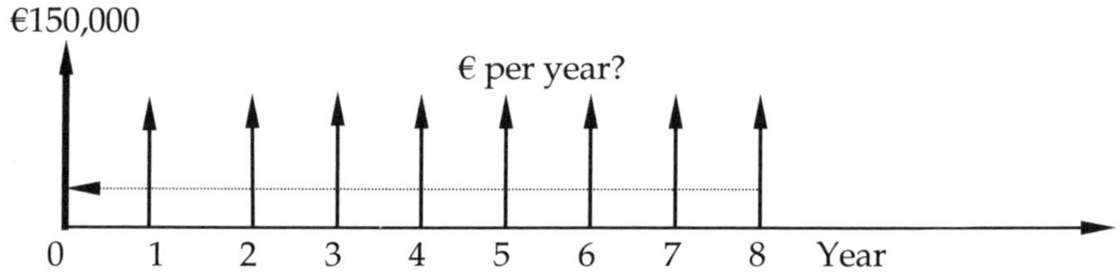

$$A = NPV_0 \cdot PVIFA_{I,N}^{-1}.$$

$$A = 150{,}000 \cdot PVIFA_{5\%,8}^{-1}.$$

$$A = 150{,}000 \cdot 0.154722 = €23{,}208.30.$$

A loan of €150,000 at 5 % interest which must be paid off in 8 years requires an annual payment of €23,208.30.

Using annuities tables

With annuities, there may be cases where NPV_0, FV_N and A are known but either the interest rate or number of time periods is unknown. From Formulas 2.10b and 2.12b we know that:

$$FVIFA_{I,N} = \frac{FV_N}{A} \quad \text{and} \quad PVIFA_{I,N} = \frac{NPV_0}{A}.$$

The unknown figure can be found using an annuity table. First, look for either $FVIFA_{I,N}$ or $PVIFA_{I,N}$ in the table by using either the interest rate or number of time periods, depending on which is given. Then, follow the table's relevant row or column until the right factor is found. This will provide the missing number. If the exact number sought does not appear in the table, locate the nearest value above and the nearest value below. Linear interpolation can then be used to determine the exact number with great precision.

Final Notes

All the above examples have been based on financing structures rather than the cash flows expected from investments in real assets. This is by design. Compared to investments in real assets, detailed calculations of net present value, future value, and interest rates can be done with much more accuracy when evaluating financial investments. This is because cash flows from investments in real assets generally are much more uncertain than financial investments and require a much higher degree of professional judgment to analyze.

The relative certainty of financial investments vis-à-vis investments in real assets leads to an important insight. It means that we should look at investments in real assets from a different perspective than we use for financial investments because the validity of cash flows and discount rate are subject to more uncertainty, and therefore greater risk.

CHAPTER 3

Capital Budgeting

One of the most important, challenging aspects of the capital budgeting process is turning the economics and technicalities of an investment strategy into a robust estimate of future cash flows. This is a demanding task, but the final cash flow projections are only as good as the business logic and accuracy of assumptions underlying them.

For each investment proposal, we need data on expected future cash flows – data which is backed up by economic, technical, and market-related sources. This data must be provided on an incremental basis so that we analyze only the difference between the company's cash flow with and without the project. This is a crucial aspect which is difficult to implement in practice because many investment projects impact other parts of the company's business.

To begin our discussion of capital budgets, we will start several notes on financing. When estimating cash flows for the investment calculation, we do not consider the cash flows related to capital financing such as disbursements, interest, financial costs, or amortizations. This is because these costs are not part of the investment's cash flow estimate itself, but rather related to the financing side of investment planning. This is a separate issue and does not enter into the calculation of whether or not the investment strategy is profitable.

The financing portion of the investment will be included only through the Weighted Average Cost of Capital (WACC), or discount rate, rather than through the cash flows related to financing. The liquidity consequences of this is an issue which should be handled separately. This subject will be covered in later chapters related to financing.

Another important insight which concerns financing is that the cash flows in a financial investment can be estimated with relative ease and precision, whereas those in real investments are inherently associated with higher degrees of uncertainty. This is because financial investments typically involve contracts (such as a bank loan) which clearly define the cash flow, but real investments are based on data analysis, choices, assumptions, estimates and, in some cases, informed guesses about the consequences of investment strategies. Therefore, the focus in this chapter will be on estimating cash flows for real investments.

The increasing sophistication of computer software and modeling tools has streamlined the preparation of cash flow projections, making them much easier and less time consuming to create. However, although computer-generated cash flow projections are powerful analytical tools, we must always remember that they are only as good as the input assumptions built into them.

Finally, it is important not to get lost in the numbers; projections are not reality. Before submitting a capital budget, we need to step back and see if the projections make sense. For instance, is it realistic to assume that a company will reach 12 % annual growth in a mature industry characterized by over-capacity?

Building the Investment Scenario

A capital budget is built from investment scenarios which a company's management has developed. These require an understanding of the drivers and parameters behind the investment decision itself, so we need to identify which factors should be included in the analysis. It is important to construct valid arguments which support the decision to exclude or include a given factor.

In order to develop sound cash flows and project assumptions, we can employ a number of classical tools used in strategic analysis. These can assist us in building solid investment scenarios and reliable estimates of future cash flows which are as realistic as possible. To do this, we must create a number of possible future situations and consider them thoroughly, evaluating the consequences for the investment project.

Our road map for creating investment scenarios is shown in the following illustration:

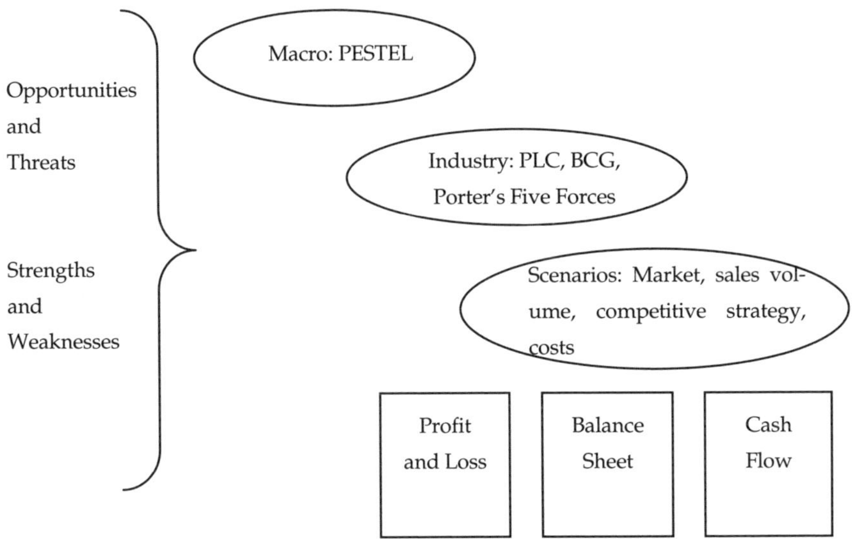

Figure 3.1 Scenario construction using strategic analysis tools

The PESTEL-model, which stands for Political, Economic, Socio-demographic, Technological, Environmental, and Legal, can be useful in creating a macro-level overview of the factors influencing the investment decision. The goal is to gain an overall picture of the changes and tendencies which can be expected and determine their potential relevance to the investment. Additionally, the PESTEL model can provide insights into how long these factors will last, which helps us identify the opportunities and threats facing the business.

The PESTEL analysis will naturally lead to a discussion of the specific industry and market where the company operates and has the ability to influence. A suitable in-depth model in this case is Michael Porter´s "Five Forces". It can be used to evaluate a particular industry's attractiveness, profitability, and return on investment. Moreover, it sheds light on the risk factors associated with each of the five forces.

When using the PESTEL and "Five Forces" models, it is important to prioritize the data received. Both models can overwhelm us with facts, so we need to skip the "nice-to-know" but unnecessary information and focus on the key factors influencing the investment decision.

An analysis of the external factors surrounding the company should be followed by a review of the internal factors which influence it. One of these is its products' stage of life. In this instance, the Product Life Cycle (PLC) tool is a robust strategic method for determining where a firm's products fall within this range. Many products follow the course of the PLC curve, with a market introduction stage, followed by periods of growth, maturity, and decline. We know from the PLC that a product's cash flow will likely be negative during the market introduction stage when production volumes are low. Sales volume and cash flow will begin to increase only during the growth stage. Then, as business risk declines, new competitors enter the market and increase the overall production capacity. This creates downward pressure on price, but the point where cash flow begins to decline depends on market dynamics and the length of the maturity stage.

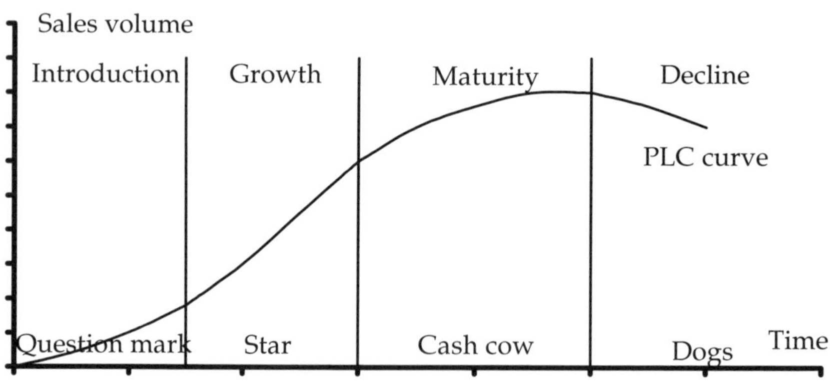

Figure 3.3 The PLC curve supplemented by cash flow over a product's life

Once maturity has ended, we can expect to see reduced cash flows as the product begins to decline. At this point, profits decrease as demand falls. This leads to excess production capacity and additional downward pressure on price

The course of the Product Life Cycle can be illustrated as shown in figure 3.3.

If a company has different product categories, their mix can be analyzed by using the Boston Consulting Group matrix (known as the BCG matrix). The BCG matrix may supplement the PLC curve and can be illustrated this way:

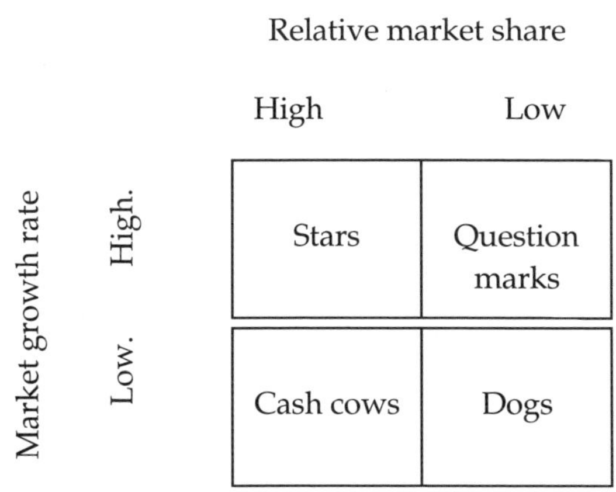

Figure 3.3 The Boston Consulting Group growth share matrix

The PLC curve's introduction stage is a parallel to the BCG matrix's "Question Marks" square, where relatively low sales volumes should rise as the market grows. The strategic focus here is on increasing sales volume and marketing the product before competitors enter the market. Ideally, this will lead the product into a growth phase, which corresponds to "Star". At this point a high market growth rate and a high market share will cause the product to dominate its field. Later, as the product enters into the mature stage, the market growth rate gradually decreases and the product becomes a "Cash cow", with a high market share but low growth rate. Ultimately, the product may enter a stage of decline as increased competition in a low-growth market drive down prices and make it become a "Dog".

The BCG matrix is a valuable tool because it highlights a product's cash flow need (or "cash burn") at different life cycle stages. The principle is that higher relative market share tends to generate cash flow. Therefore, "Stars" and particularly "Question marks" require cash, but "Dogs" and especially "Cash cows" generate positive cash flow.

The PLC curve and the BCG matrix illustrate how investment projects evolve through stages of varying cash flow requirements. We can use this knowledge to develop well-considered cash flow estimates for our investment projects in question.

Any strategic analysis naturally leads to decisions about competitive strategies and scenarios for the investment project. The more uncertain variables there are, the more scenarios we will have to consider.

As previously mentioned, the key element in the above analysis is to consider and evaluate a number of possible investment outcomes. Doing so will enable us to construct solid investment strategies and reliable cash flow estimates, all based on reasonable arguments and assumptions. Among the most important aspects to cover are market size, market share, revenues, costs, company resources required, and the competitive situation.

Cash flow estimation

The information discussed above will lay the foundation for estimating the investment strategy's cash flows. When doing this, we typically look at three sets of estimates:

1) Income statement.
2) Balance sheet.
3) Statement of cash flows.

The connection between these estimates is specified in the assumptions (for example, credit to debtors, stock turnover, tax, depreciation schedules, etc). In conducting investment analysis we focus on *incremental cash flows*. Therefore, we will not use the estimates of revenue and expenditures seen in the profit and loss accounts, but rather look at the incremental cash inflows and outflows which can be expected. This distinction is particularly important when it comes to depreciation because this is an allocation of costs related to asset investments which is spread over time. Depreciations are a financial accounting tool and therefore do not form part of the cash flow estimation.

Two principal issues should be mentioned with regard to cash flow estimation:

1) *Opportunity costs* should be included in the calculation if the investment leads to a loss of existing or alternative income.
2) *Sunk costs* are irreversible and should not be included in the investment analysis. These may include research and development costs, or other costs incurred before a project is under consideration for execution.

Ideally, cash flow estimates can be structured by considering the following five elements:

1. Capital expenditures/initial investment.
2. Financing.
3. Sales.
4. Costs.
5. Assumptions.

Capital expenditures/initial investments
This may take several forms, including land, buildings, equipment, pre-operational costs, and training costs. Other potential items include necessary working capital for accounts receivable, raw material stocks, work-in-progress inventory, finished goods inventory, and cash on hand. Cash outlays for these initial investments may be staged over a number of years, and this should be considered in the cash flow estimation. Practical experience shows that cost overruns occur quite frequently, so a prudent investment analysis always includes a buffers for miscellaneous costs.

Estimating the initial investment's needs and capital expenditures is a demanding task which requires a number of decisions to be made, including:

- Capacity needs.
- Economies of scale.
- Investment phases.
- New or used equipment/buildings.
- Purchase, rent, or lease.
- Re-investments.
- Surrounding infrastructure.

This capital expenditures/initial investments portion of the capital budgeting process includes estimating the project's scrap or terminal value at the end of the investment's time horizon. In simple cases, the scrap value is merely the salvage value of the equipment, plus the recovery of working capital. In other instances, there may be equipment disposal costs, such as with an oil rig that must be dismantled when exploration ends. In this case, the scrap value would be the difference between the selling price of the obsolete oil rig and the cost of dismantling it.

In many capital budgeting situations, the project in question will continue beyond the investment time horizon. Here, the challenge is to capture the value of cash flows which occur after our time horizon has ended. We can calculate this terminal value by assuming that the cash flow estimated at Time t, CF_t, will continue indefinitely. This would mean that N=@, and the net present value of this infinite cash flow stream would be CF_t divided by the discount rate, I. We can modify this by adding an estimate, g, for the anticipated growth rate in the project's cash flow. When we add this growth rate, the terminal value at the end of Time t, TV_t, will equal:

$$TV_t = \frac{CF_t}{I - g} \tag{3.1}$$

Example 3.1
Suppose we have set a five-year time horizon on an investment project we are evaluating. We know that the project will continue longer, following the trend seen over the first five years. The cash flow at t=5 is estimated at €200,000 and we expect it to continue growing at 10 % per year. With a discount rate of 25 %, the terminal value at t=5 of would be:

$$TV_5 = \frac{200{,}000}{0.25 - 0.1} = €1{,}333{,}333\,.$$

Discounting this terminal value back to time t=0 yields:

$$\text{NPV}_0\,(\text{TV}) = \text{TV}_5 \cdot (1 + 25\ \%)^{-5} = 1{,}333{,}333 \cdot (1 + 25\ \%)^{-5} = €436{,}907.$$

Financing
As mentioned previously, cash flows from financing do not enter the investment analysis directly. However, financing decisions impact the investment analysis through the WACC, so financing should be considered because it is very important to liquidity. Financing is explored in more detail in future chapters.

Key elements to consider in terms of financing are:

- Amount of debt compared to equity.
- Availability of various types of financing.
- Possibilities for refinancing.
- Lending environment.
- Effective cost of capital / WACC.

Sales
The estimation of sales is basically a question of price and volumes. Preparing this estimate is a complicated but crucial part of the investment case, especially when there is no historical data at hand. Analytical tools and structures which can be used in this connection are:

- Price optimization.
- Porter's "Five Forces".
- Market forms/competitive rivalry.
- Product Life Cycle.
- Price/income elasticities.
- Market positioning.

Costs
Cash flow estimates are always concerned with operational costs, which typically involve variable costs, semi-variable costs, and fixed costs. Costing is linked to sales estimation and usually reflects the following factors:

- Raw materials.
- Packaging.
- Salaries and wages.
- Energy.
- Repair and maintenance.
- Sales and marketing.
- Administration.

Assumptions
This portion of the capital budget includes a listing of all the underlying investment project assumptions which influence actual cash flow. Depending on the specific project at hand, assumptions may either have a small or significant impact on cash flow. In any case, it is important that the investment analysis phase lists the assumptions made to test their robustness and validity. For instance, assumptions could be about:

- Tax.
- Depreciation.
- Credit periods.
- Inventories.
- Consequences for sales of other products.

The final item in this list, consequences for sales of other products, should include the investment's positive or negative effects on other aspects of the company's business, such as its impact on the sales of existing products.

With the estimates for capital expenditures/initial investments, financing, sales, costs and assumptions now in hand, we have a basis for estimating the cash flows of a company's investment scenarios.

CHAPTER 4

Optimal Investment Horizon and Replacement

Economic and Technical Lifespan

Up until now, we have assumed that an investment project's lifespan was a known parameter. In this chapter, we relax that assumption and will let the investment's lifespan be a variable that we optimize according to when the net present value is maximized.

We define the investment time-frame which maximizes net present value as the *economic lifespan*. The optimal lifespan is reached when NPV has been maximized, and the number of time periods n is the controlling variable:

$$\boldsymbol{Max} \quad \boldsymbol{NPV}_0 = \sum_{t=0}^{n} \boldsymbol{CF}_t \cdot (1 + \boldsymbol{I})^{-t}.$$

$$\boldsymbol{n} = 0,1,2\ldots, \boldsymbol{T}$$

The economic lifespan n will be less than or equal to the maximum period in which the investment can technically operate. This is called the *technical lifespan*, or T.

There can be several reasons why the economic lifespan may be less than the technical lifespan:

1. The investment might be made in products or markets that will eventually enter into a declining part of their product life cycle. In such a situation, the marginal cost of operation may exceed the

marginal revenues, making it worthwhile to alter operations or cease them altogether.

2. Another situation is where the marginal costs of operation, maintenance, and repair increase over time, to the point that it becomes more cost-effective to replace the existing equipment with new in order to reduce the long-term average cost.
3. A third situation is the case where technological advances result in better and more cost-effective equipment becoming available, which lets unit costs be reduced by replacing existing equipment with newer versions.

These three situations and their related decision analyses can be summarized as:

1. *Economic lifespan* of a one-time investment, where replacement after the time period ends is not a consideration.
2. *Identical replacement,* in which equipment will be replaced with something identical, in a long (infinite) chain of investments.
3. *Replacement with new and better equipment,* where existing equipment is replaced with a different and better version.

Economic Lifespan of a Single Investment

Underlying the *economic lifespan* for a single, non-repeated investment is the classical marginal reasoning of managerial economics. Here, the marginal approach is to continue the investment for a given time period only if the marginal revenue exceeds the marginal cost of continuing operations. Once marginal costs become greater than marginal revenue, it no longer makes economic sense to continue the investment, so the rational decision is to stop. This is the point when NPV has been maximized with regard to economic lifespan.

There is an important distinction between the marginal approach described above and investment theory's emphasis strictly on cash flow: the marginal approach operates with *economic costing,* whereas investment calculations consider only the direct and actual cash inflows and outflows. Economic costs include both the direct cash flows and the possible opportunity cost. The opportunity cost is defined as *the value foregone by committing to a given course of action, as this may preclude alternative actions.* Opportunity costs may also be referred to as alternative costs. This is because they take into account the costs incurred as a result of a particular choice, when a different choice would have given an alternative value.

This latter value is the alternative or opportunity cost.

The economic costs which we will consider for each period of a given investment are as follows:

1. *The value lost* by holding assets:
    - The market value of an asset will typically decrease over time as it ages in each period. One component of the value lost by holding the asset for one period is therefore the decrease in worth related to its age.
    - By using the asset during the period, it will suffer a certain amount of wear and tear. Therefore another component of the value lost by holding and using the asset for one period is the decrease in worth related to how it is used and maintained.

   The value lost by holding the asset for one period is often expressed as the period's depreciation. However, in accounting terms depreciation is determined primarily by tax legislation and therefore does not necessarily reflect the true value lost by holding the asset for that period.
2. *The opportunity cost in the form of lost interest.* The money dedicated to a given production asset might alternatively have been invested in bonds or a similar interest-bearing vehicle. By committing available finances to a production facility, a company must forego the return on bonds. This return, or interest, is an opportunity cost.

3. *Operation and maintenance.* Running a production facility entails operating and maintenance costs, which typically increase as the equipment ages.
4. *Other costs.* There are a variety of costs unique to each situation which might be direct or indirect, as well as related opportunity costs.

We can develop the following table to calculate the optimal economic life-span:

Period	**0**	**1**	**2**	.....
Scrap value				
Value loss				
Interest loss				
Operation & maintenance costs				
Other costs				
Total marginal costs (MC)				
Marginal revenue (MR)				
Marginal revenue – Marginal costs				
Period's NPV				
Accumulated NPV				

In this table, the input variables are:

Period	Period number. This will usually be years, but may be any time period relevant for the analysis
Scrap value	Realized value of the asset at end of the period
Value loss	Change in realized value between the previous period and end of the period in question

Interest loss	The opportunity interest or return the company could have had by divesting itself of the asset and investing its money in interest-bearing assets
Operation and maintenance costs	The costs of running and maintaining the asset during the period
Other costs	All other direct, indirect, or opportunity costs which can be attributed to using the asset for the period
Total marginal costs	The sum of value loss, interest loss, operation and maintenance costs, and other costs
Marginal revenue	Marginal revenue from operating during the period
Marginal revenue minus total marginal costs	Net amount remaining after subtracting the period's total marginal costs from marginal revenue
Period's NPV	Net present value of the period's marginal revenue minus total marginal costs
Accumulated NPV	Accumulated net present values of all periods up to period "n"

The optimal economic lifespan is determined as the time when the "Marginal revenue minus total marginal costs" changes from a positive to negative value. (This assumes that the accumulated NPV exceeds zero; if it does not exceed zero, the project should be stopped immediately).

Example 4.1

A new manufacturing facility where a new product will be fabricated has an initial capital investment of €2,000,000. The facility depreciates at 30 % per year according to the balance method and can be sold at any time for book value. Operation and maintenance costs are projected to be €125,000 during the first year and to rise by 15 % in each year of use thereafter. The facility's marginal revenue is forecast at €750,000 in the first year, but will likely decrease by 9 % p.a. in the following years due to increased competition. The firm uses a discount rate of 10 % p.a. and has alternative investment options which will earn this rate of return each year. Should the company commit to this investment strategy? If so, what is the optimal amount of time for it to remain in the market?

To find the solution we complete the investment table using the data provided. We see that the proposed strategy would lead to net losses in each of the first two years, but afterwards turn around. Consequently, the annual NPV is positive from Year 3 to Year 7, with a maximum marginal profit of €103,606 in the fifth year. After Year 7, however, annual profits decline because of lower revenues and increased maintenance and operating costs. Although profit levels are decreasing NPV is still positive in Years 6 and 7, so accumulated NPV continues to grow until Year 8.

The initial decision to make is whether or not this investment strategy is worth pursuing in the first place. Does the accumulated NPV justify committing capital and resources, given the risk to be taken? The calculations show that *if* a decision is made to engage in this investment strategy, the optimal lifespan is approximately 7 to 8 years. Year 7 returns a positive net amount when subtracting marginal revenue from total marginal costs, and therefore also a positive NPV. Year 8 results in a minor loss. If the investment strategy in pursued for seven years, the investment's accumulated NPV will be maximized at about €72,600.

Period	0	1	2	3	4	5	6
Scrap val.	2,000,000	1,400,000	980,000	686,000	480,000	336,140	234,298
Value loss		600,000	420,000	294,000	205,800	144,060	100,842
Lost interest		200,000	140,000	98,000	68,600	48,020	33,614
Oper. & mainten.		125,000	143,750	165,313	190,109	218,626	251,420
Total MC		925,000	703,750	557,313	464,509	410,706	385,876
MR		750,000	682,500	621,075	565,178	514,312	468,024
MR–MC		–175,000	–21,250	63,763	100,669	103,606	82,148
NPV		–159,091	–17,562	47,906	68,758	64,331	46,371
Acc NPV		–159,091	–176,653	–128,747	–59,989	4,342	50,713

Period	*7*	**8**	**9**	**10**	**11**	**12**
Scrap value	***164,709***	115,296	80,707	56,495	39,547	27,683
Value loss	***70,589***	49,413	34,589	24,212	16,949	11,864
Lost interest	***23,530***	16,471	11,530	8,071	5,650	3,955
Ops. & maintenance	***289,133***	332,502	382,378	439,735	505,695	581,549
Total marginal cost	***383,252***	398,386	428,496	472,017	528,293	597,368
MR	***425,902***	387,571	352,689	320,947	292,062	265,777
MR–MC	***42,650***	–10,815	–75,807	–151,070	–236,231	–331,591
NPV	***21,886***	–5,045	–32,149	–58,245	–82,797	–105,656
Acc NPV	***72,599***	67,554	35,405	–22,840	–105,637	–211,292

The development can be graphically illustrated as follows:

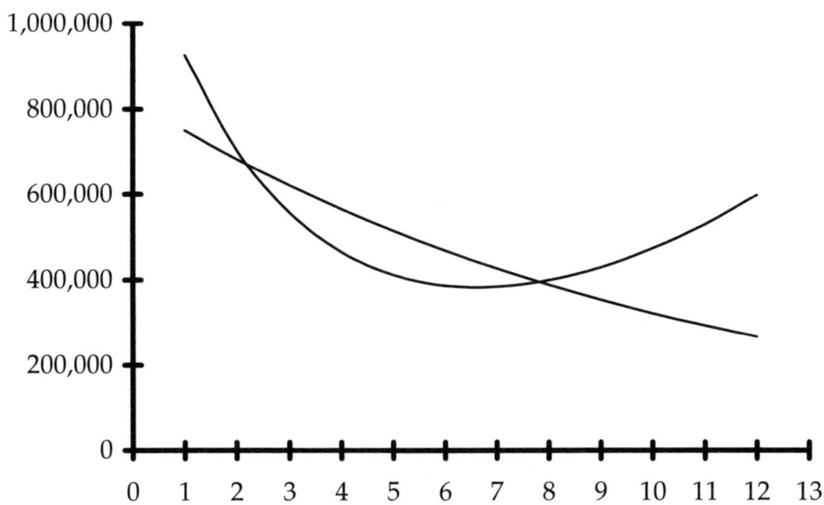

Figure 4.1 Economic lifespan

The graph shows that the total marginal costs are larger than the marginal revenue for the first two years, followed by several years where the marginal revenue exceeds marginal costs. Therefore the investment project is profitable over this time period.

Marginal revenue and marginal cost intersect at approximately 7.4 years. If the firm remains in operation after this point it will continue losing money and the investment will eventually become unprofitable.

Another way to approach this is to look at the accumulated net present value and end the project when it has reached its highest value.

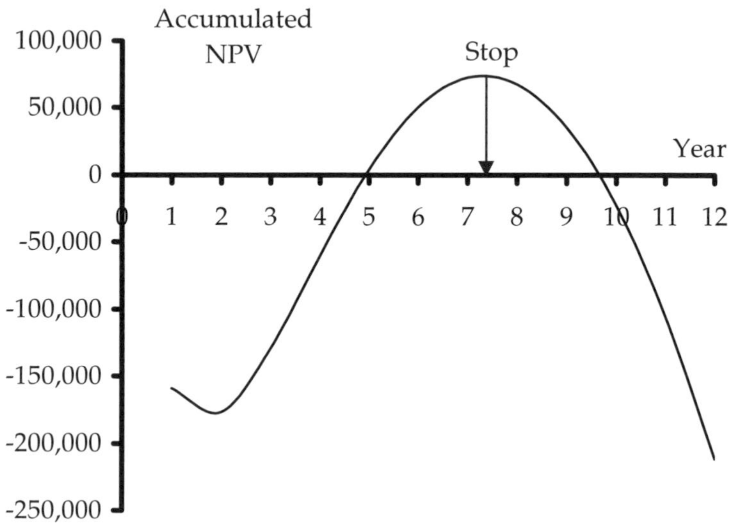

Figure 4.2 Economic lifespan

Identical Replacement

Identical replacement is based on the assumption of successive investments in identical equipment. It is an approach often used in the absence of better and more realistic expectations about the future. In this case, we operate with the single individual investment as the basis and assume that replacement investments are made in an infinite chain. The analysis is concerned with identifying the optimal lifespan of the initial, basic investment.

This lifespan will be the one which yields the highest possible return for the entire chain since the replacement investments will have the same duration. In many cases, when considering identical replacements, we take only the costs into account, assuming that revenues will remain the same after each replacement. In these cases we look at the lifespan which yields the lowest possible cost.

The total net present value of an infinite chain of annual annuities provided by the basic investment can be calculated as:

$$NPV_{0\,,\,Chain\ of\ identical\ investments} = \frac{A_{Basic\ investment}}{I}\,.$$

Because the discount rate, I, is fixed, the net present value of identical investments in similar assets is maximized when the basic investment's annuity, A, is maximized. If we are only looking at costs, we can maximize the investment by reducing their net present value to the optimum level. This occurs at the point where the negative annuity of the basic investment is minimized.

This analysis is facilitated by listing the data in a table. The scheme for *identical replacement* resembles the one used for economic lifespan. The only change is that we add a column for the annuity because by optimizing this we maximize the net present value of the entire chain of identical replacements:

Period	0	1	2	.....
Scrap value				
Value loss				
Interest loss				
Operation & maintenance costs				
Other costs				
Total marginal costs				
Marginal revenue				
Marginal revenue – Marginal costs				
Period's NPV				
Accumulated NPV				
Annuity				

The annuity represents the average net cash flow per time period.

If costs-only are considered, then the columns with "Marginal revenue" and "Marginal revenue – Marginal costs" can be eliminated and the NPV calculation will be based on only costs. In this case the annuity will have to be minimized rather than maximized.

Example 4.2

A company wants to analyze the optimal replacement policy for one of their production facilities. Since the revenue side is considered independent from the cost side, only costs are taken into consideration.

The new facility will cost €1,500,000, and, lacking better information as to possible future alternatives, management is operating under an assumption of identical replacements.

For simplicity, the facility is expected to depreciate at 30 % per year according to the balance method and can be sold at any time for book value. It is technologically advanced, with high repair and maintenance costs that will increase over time. These are estimated at €100,000 in the first year and will rise by 30 % per year. The company can place its money elsewhere at any time and generate a rate of return of 10 % p.a.

Each annuity is calculated by taking the accumulated net present value at each time period and spreading it over the total number of time periods during which the cash flow has been generated. The annuity for Period 2 is therefore calculated as:

$$A_2 = NPV_2 \cdot PVIFA^{-1}_{10\%,2} = 1{,}090{,}909 \cdot 0.576 = 628{,}571.$$

and the annuity for Period 3 as:

$$A_3 = NPV_3 \cdot \boldsymbol{PVIFA^{-1}_{10\%,3}} = 1{,}438{,}768 \cdot 0.402 = 578{,}550.$$

and so forth.

Period	**0**	**1**	**2**	**3**	**4**
Scrap value	1,500,000	1,050,000	735,000	514,500	360,150
Value loss		450,000	315,000	220,500	154,350
Lost interest		150,000	105,000	73,500	51,450
Operation & maintenance		100,000	130,000	169,000	219,700
Total marginal cost		700,000	550,000	463,000	425,500
NPV		636,364	454,545	347,859	290,622
Acc NPV		636,364	1,090,909	1,438,768	1,729,390
Annuity		700,000	628,571	578,550	545,572

Period	**5**	**6**	**7**	**8**	**9**
Scrap value	252,105	***176,474***	123,531	86,472	60,530
Value loss	108,045	***75,632***	52,942	37,059	25,942
Lost interest	36,015	***25,211***	17,647	12,353	8,647
Operation & maintenance	285,610	***371,293***	482,681	627,485	815,731
Total marginal cost	429,670	***472,135***	553,270	676,898	850,320
NPV	266,791	***266,508***	283,915	315,778	360,618
Acc NPV	1,996,181	***2,262,689***	2,546,604	2,862,382	3,223,001
Annuity	526,588	***519,530***	523,087	536,536	559,644

The table shows that yearly cost is lowest in Year 4 at €425,500. However, when we discount costs back to the beginning of Year 0 and convert them into an annuity of yearly average costs, the minimum average annual cost of €519,530 is achieved in Year 6. The optimal replacement policy is therefore to replace the production facility every six years. This will reduce the annuity of average cost to its lowest possible value, which minimizes the negative NPV of a chain of identical replacements. This can be illustrated as in figure 4.3.

The calculations and the following graph show that the precise time of optimal replacement is not critical. Whether the replacement takes place in Year 5, 6 or 7 will not make much difference because the change in the average annual cost is only 1.5 % over this three-year period. Thus it is sufficient to calculate the optimal replacement time in approximate terms since the marginal benefit of defining the time exactly is typically very small.

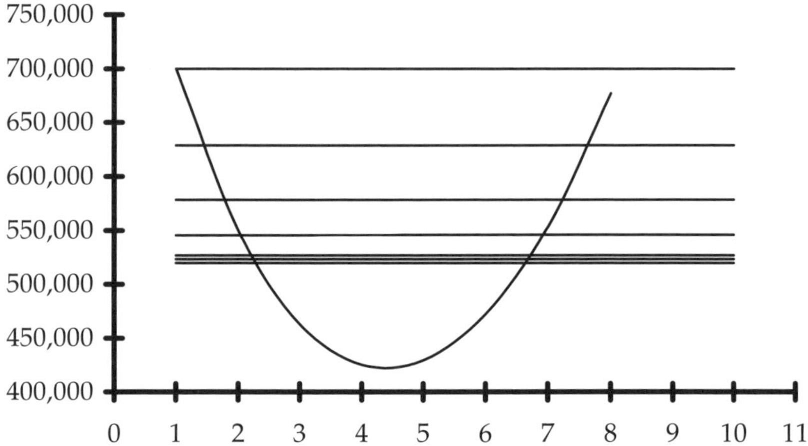

Figure 4.3 Identical replacement

In some situations, cost elements will cancel each other out. For instance, in the previous example, there is a decreasing value loss and loss of interest year over year, but maintenance and repair costs are increasing. The chosen solution will typically be influenced very little by deviations from the exact optimal replacement solution.

Replacing Existing Equipment with New and Better

Replacement of existing equipment with new and better equipment occurs when the existing facility is no longer available on the market, or when newer and more cost-efficient alternatives are available. The challenge in this case is to find the optimal replacement time.

This is done by combining the two previous methods. Typically we will focus on costs, as in the case above, since revenues are assumed to be independent from the analysis of equipment. First we must decide on an optimal replacement policy for the new and better equipment in accordance with the identical replacement method. From this, we determine the new equipment's lowest possible average cost per period.

Then we compare the average annual cost of the new equipment to the marginal cost of the existing equipment. As long as the marginal cost of the existing equipment is less than the average annual cost of the new equipment, there is no need to replace it. However, when the cost per period for the existing equipment is greater than the minimum average cost per period for the new equipment, we should make a replacement.

Example 4.3
A firm has equipment similar to that described in Example 4.1. The equipment is three years old, but can technically be used for many more years. However, management believes that the new equipment described in Example 4.2 is more cost-efficient and technologically advanced, and it would like to determine the best timing for replacing its existing equipment.

The marginal yearly cost for the existing equipment was calculated in Example 4.1 to be:

Year	Total cost per year
0	
1	925.000
2	703,750
3	557,313
4	464,509
5	410,706
6	385,876
7	383,252
8	398,386
9	428,496
10	472,017
11	528,293
12	597,368

Meanwhile, from Example 4.2, we know that the minimum average cost per year for the new equipment is €519,530 on a six-year basis.

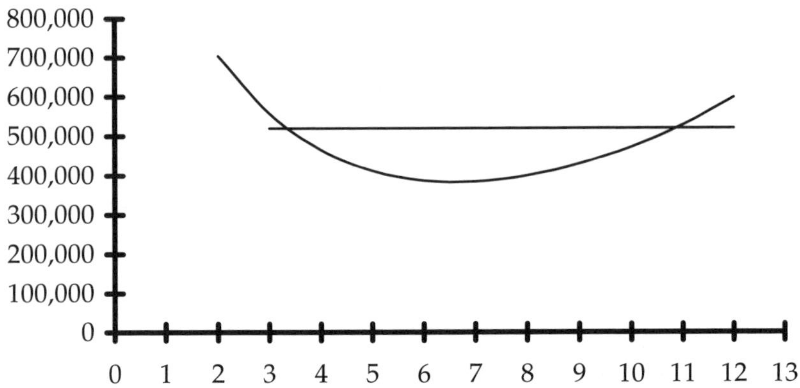

Figure 4.4 Replacement of equipment with new and better.

Because the existing facility is already three years old, we can ignore the costs pertaining to this period because even though they are greater than the benchmark (€557,313 vs. €519,530), they have already been incurred. From the fourth year onward, the total yearly cost for the old equipment is less than the minimum average cost for the new equipment. *Not until Year 11 does the existing equipment's marginal yearly cost exceed the minimum annual average cost of the new equipment.* It is at this point that the replacement should be done.

CHAPTER 5

Financial Evaluation of Investments

Evaluating Single and Alternative Investments

In this chapter we will discuss the best means to evaluate a single investment strategy on its own, as well as compare alternative investments in cases where more than one option exists. Alternative investments often have differences in their time horizons and capital requirements, so we will look at these issues in detail.

Single Investments

The simplest investment decision is one where an individual project is being evaluated, which the investor can accept or reject. This type of investment must not be dependent upon previous investments which now require further decisions and capital. Similarly, no supplementary investments are involved. Instead, the opportunity represents a one-time commitment of capital which is independent of the past and places no constraint on the future. An example would be a small manufacturing company which has traditionally used a logistics services provider to deliver its goods but is now contemplating buying its own delivery truck. If the company decides to make the investment, it will not be restricted from selling the truck in the future or using the contractor again. It may even, if it wishes, do something altogether different.

The criteria for determining if an independent investment is advantageous is that its net present value be greater than 0. This is the same as saying it will add value to the company or investor by increasing shareholder value.

At a given discount rate, an investment is profitable if its net present value is greater than zero.

The alternative to a single investment is that no funds are committed to the project – i.e., that a "zero investment" is made. The inference is that available capital will be invested at the discount rate, where the net present value is zero and shareholder value does not increase.

Investment theory typically uses three primary measures to evaluate the profitability of investments:

- Net present value.
- Internal rate of return.
- Annuity.

When evaluating a single investment, these three methods will always lead to the same result in terms of the investment's being profitable or not.

In the pages which follow, we will discuss each one in turn and use a number of examples and situations to illustrate their proper application.

The Net Present Value

The shareholder value principle is applied directly in the net present value method, where the investment is said to be profitable only if its net present value is greater than zero.

Example 5.1
Let us consider an investment of €100,000 which will generate a positive cash flow of €30,000 per year over the next five years:

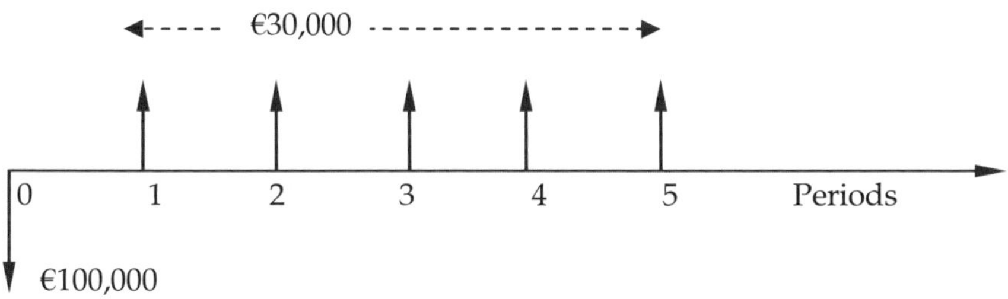

The net present value can be determined from the following equation:

$$NPV_0 = -100{,}000 + 30{,}000 \cdot PVIFA_{I,N}$$

It is important to note that the value of NPV_0 will vary according to the project discount rate which is used. For instance, if it is set at 10 % per year in this example, NPV_0 will be approximately €13,700 and the investment will be profitable. However, if it is fixed at 20 % per year NPV_0 decreases to –€10,300, and the investment should not be made. Therefore a project's degree of profitability is dependent on the investor's required rate of return, as measured by the discount rate which is used.

All things being equal, investments are generally more profitable when the discount rate is lower rather than higher. This is because expected future cash flows have a smaller net present value at higher discount rates. Consequently, strategic and long-term investments are usually more feasible in situations where the discount rate is relatively low.

The Internal Rate of Return

In addition to determining the net present value of an investment, we can also calculate its internal rate of return on invested capital. This is defined as follows:

The internal rate of return of an investment is the rate of return which yields a net present value of precisely 0.

This can be expressed by the following equation:

$$NPV_0 = 0 = \sum_{t=0} CF_t \cdot (1 + IRR)^{-t}.$$

IRR is the internal rate of return which will yield the result $NPV_0 = 0$. It therefore represents the discount rate which makes the net present value of all discounted future cash flows equal to zero. Consequently, in an investment which yields a positive net present value at a given discount rate, we can gradually increase the discount rate until the NPV becomes zero. It is at this point, where the discount rate yields a net present value of zero, that we find the internal rate of return.

As can be seen, the equation given above is of the tth degree. Such equations are hard to solve with long-hand arithmetic, so we typically use a financial calculator or spreadsheet to find an investment's IRR.

In Example 5.1 we saw that a discount rate of 10 % p.a. yields a positive net present value of approximately €13,700. We also realized that increasing it to 20 % p.a. causes the net present value to become negative, with a return of –€10,300. This means that if we gradually increase the discount rate from 10 % p.a. to 20 % p.a., there must be a point along this continuum where the net present value is zero. This is where we will have increased our required rate of return, or discount rate, to such a level that the project is no longer profitable and the net present value becomes zero. We can illustrate this relationship between the discount rate and the net present value graphically as follows:

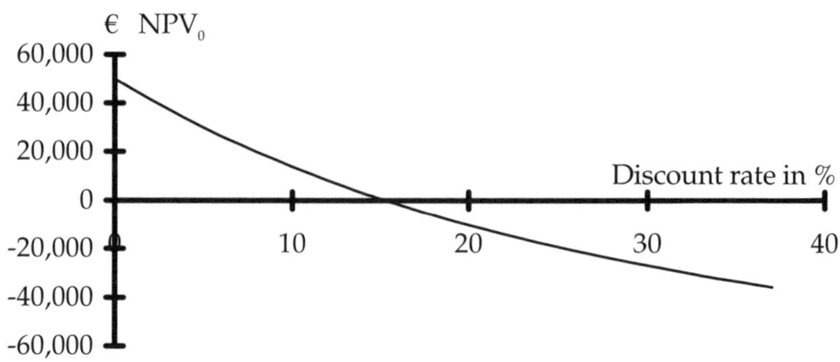

Figure 5.1 Net present value as a function of the discount rate

From Figure 5.1 we see that a discount rate of less than 15 % per year (or 15.24 %, to be exact) will yield a positive net present value, whereas one below this figure will yield a negative net present value. NPV is positive as long as the IRR exceeds the investors' required return as defined by the discount rate, because the project adds value by returning more on their invested capital than their threshold has required.

A discount rate of approximately 15 % per year, where the investment's net present value changes sign from positive to negative, is exactly the return which its invested capital obtains. For this reason the corresponding discount rate is called the *internal rate of return*, or *IRR*.

We can express this formally as:

An investment is profitable if its internal rate of return is larger than the applied discount rate.

The significance of IRR is that it provides a point of reference for determining an investment's profitability. In particular, investments are profitable and add value only when they yield a higher return than the minimum percentage required in the form of the discount rate.

It should be noted that the internal rate of return on an investment is generated only on the money actually out-of-pocket at any point in time. Thus, the IRR is not generated on the original investment amount during the investment period if a cash return has been realized, but on the unreturned capital still outstanding. We can illustrate this with the cash flow from Example 3.1, where the internal rate of return was calculated as 15.24 % p.a. Applying this rate to the project's capital balance at the end of each period makes the net present value equal 0 after exactly five periods.

Period	Invested Capital at beginning of period	Interest accrued at an interest rate of 15,24 % p.a.	Cash Outflow from Project	Invested Capital at end of period
1	100,000	15,238	30,000	85,238
2	85,238	12,989	30,000	68,227
3	68,227	10,397	30,000	48,624
4	48,624	7,409	30,000	26,033
5	26,033	3,967	30,000	0

The table above illustrates that the €100,000 initially invested earns an interest (or return) of 15.24 % (€15,238) during Period 1. Cash inflow to the investor during Period 1 is €30,000, leaving €85,238 still invested at its conclusion. It is this lower amount of invested capital that is again earning 15.24 % interest during Period 2, which is equivalent to €12,989. As before, there is a €30,000 cash inflow during Period 2, so the invested money at the end of it is €68,227, and so forth. Overall, we see that applying a discount rate of 15.24 % p.a. will leave us with exactly 0 invested at the end of the investment's horizon.

If the cash flow has more than one sign change – as might be the case if the investment leads to additional net cash inflows in future periods – the internal rate of return may become ambiguous. Indeed, there will be as many internal rates of return as there are sign changes in the cash flow. Consequently, the internal rate of return method is not suitable forr cash flows with fluctuating signs. In cases with multiple internal rates of return, it is common practice to use the lowest IRR value as the internal rate of return.

Example 5.2
A manufacturing company has the option to make an investment of €200,000 which would increase its cash flow by €650,000 per year over a period of two years. However, at the end of the second year, the company must dismantle the entire production facility and renovate it for a cost of €1,150,000. Should the company make the investment?

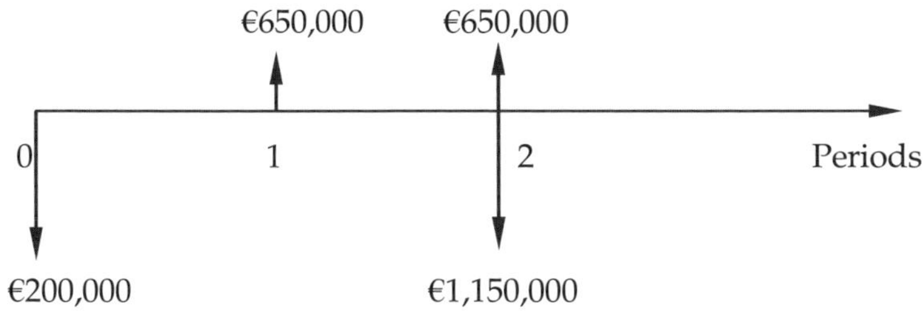

Figure 5.2 illustrates the relationship between the investment project's discount rate and its net present value. If the discount rate is below 25 % p.a., the net present value will be negative; if it falls between 25 % p.a. and 100 % p.a., the net present value will be positive. Lastly, if the discount rate is set above 100 % p.a., the net present value will again turn negative.

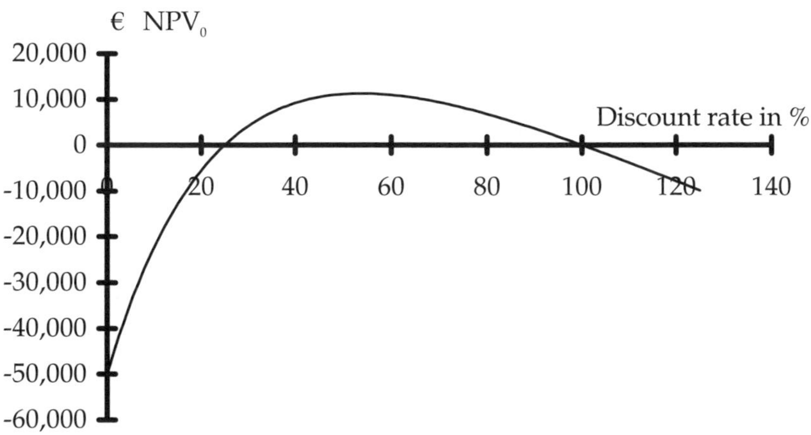

Figure 5.2 An investment with more than one internal rate of return

From this example we see that using different discount rates will yield very different results. Let us assume that the discount rate we apply is the market interest rate, that is, the interest rate where borrowing and lending of capital can be done freely. We will also assume that the project is financed entirely by debt borrowed at this market interest rate. Finally, we will assume that all surplus capital is able to earn the market rate. When we then apply different market interest rates, we will see different cash flows and results as illustrated below:

Period	Start of period	Interest	Revenue	End of period
1	–200,000	–20,000	650,000	430,000
2	430,000	43,000	–500,000	–27,000

This table shows that the investment will generate a loss of €27,000 at the end of two years. This because the cash balance which exists at the beginning of Year 2, combined with the interest it will earn during the second year, is not sufficient to cover the second year loss. However, if the market interest rate is set at 50 % p.a., a different picture emerges:

Period	Start of period	Interest	Revenue	End of period
1	–200,000	–100,000	650,000	350,000
2	350,000	175,000	–500,000	25,000

Even though the cash balance at the beginning of the second year is less than it was before, the market interest rate is now so high that the cash balance plus the second year's interest is large enough to cover the corresponding period deficit. If the market interest rate reaches a level of 150 % (an extreme situation), we would again see a negative result after the second year:

Period	Start of period	Interest	Revenue	End of period
1	–200,000	–300,000	650,000	150,000
2	150,000	225,000	–500,000	–125,000

The reason is that the Year 1 interest cost consumes such a large portion part of annual revenues that the remaining balance, even when earning 150 % interest rate over the course of Year 2, does not cover that year's loss.

The Annuity

The annuity is an investment measure which indicates how much cash outflow will be generated in each period if the net present value is spread in equal amounts over the investment's lifetime. In order to derive the annuity value which covers the lifetime of the investment, we must first calculate the net present value. Then we convert the NPV into a number of equal annuities by multiplying it by an amortization factor which equals the reciprocal of the Present Value Interest Factor of an Annuity, or $\boldsymbol{PVIFA_{I,N}^{-1}}$

$$A = NPV_0 \cdot \boldsymbol{PVIFA_{I,N}^{-1}}.$$

As a reciprocal number, the amortization factor will take on a value between 0 and 1, which means that the annuity will have the same sign as the investment's net present value. In other words, if the net present value is positive the annuity will also be positive, and if it is negative the annuity will also be negative. Because an investment is profitable only if the net present value is positive, we can conclude that:

An investment is profitable if its annuity is positive.

Returning to the net present values given in Example 5.1, if we convert these sums into annuities, a discount rate of 10 % per year will yield an annuity of €3,620. Consequently, the investment is profitable at a discount rate of 10 % per year. If the discount rate is increased to 20 % per year, however, the annuity becomes –€3,438, at which point the investment is seen to be unprofitable.

Based on the examples and calculations provided above, we can conclude that when NPV, IRR, and annuities are used to evaluate the profitability of a single investment, which starts with a payment in the first period and is followed by a number of cash inflows, they all lead to the same conclusion. The key can be summarized as:

Single Investments

	Net Present Value	Internal Rate of Return	Annuity
Applicability	Always	Only one sign change	Always
Decision Criteria	NPV ≥ 0	IRR ≥ Discount rate	Annuity ≥ 0

Alternative Investments

The decision-making process for investments becomes more complex when a choice must be made between alternative investments which can either be interrelated or mutually exclusive. If the investments are interrelated, the extent to which they influence one another – whether positively or negatively – must be determined. After this is done, we can list the investment alternatives and begin to compare them.

Interrelated investments imply that one of the alternatives' cash flow is influenced by whether or not the other investment is also undertaken. For example, if a choice must be made between two investment alternatives, A and B, and B's cash flow would be altered if an investment were also made in A, this would give rise to three mutually exclusive alternatives: 1) invest in A only; 2) invest in B only; or 3) invest in both A and B.

A situation arose where Alternative B depended upon a simultaneous investment in Alternative A, but where an investment in A would not necessarily lead to an investment in B, there would be two mutually exclusive alternatives: 1) invest in A only; or 2) invest in both A and B.

In the following sections we will examine how to apply the net present value, internal rate of return, and annuity methods when evaluating alternative investments. Two very important questions now come into play:

- Is it significant that the investment amounts are different?
- Is it significant that the investments have different lifespans?

Net Present Value

From a shareholder value perspective, the reason for making strategic investments is to maximize net present value for the investor or company. Therefore, when companies are faced with decision alternatives they naturally prefer the investment which yields the highest net present value. This can be stated as follows:

The most profitable investment out of a number of mutually exclusive options is the one with the highest net present value.

When calculating net present value, the amount of initial capital expenditure should be directly included. This means that investments with different amounts of expenditures will generate different NPVs. The investment with the highest NPV is the one which maximizes shareholder value, regardless of the initial capital's expenditure's size. Therefore the net present value method correctly ranks alternative investments having different initial amounts.

The above discussion assumes that financing is freely available to fund the initial investment. If it is not, however, or if the alternatives are not mutually exclusive, we may have to use capital rationing. This need may also arise if the company has questions about the amounts to be invested, such as if a smaller investment with a lower NPV were to have a greater percentage gain than a higher-NPV alternative.

The goal of capital rationing is to help a company determine the best way to allocate financial resources among investment opportunities, given a set of limiting constraints. The need may be self-imposed or externally driven. Self-imposed capital rationing may occur when a company, needing to steward its resources carefully, seeks to avoid raising new debt or equity for an investment. Another instance is when it operates in a time of strategic uncertainty and is unable to commit resources or management time to all of the opportunities before it. In such cases the company chooses to limit its capital expenditure plans and budgets.

External capital rationing, meanwhile, occurs when a company with less access to financing is denied capital expenditure funding, either because banks are unwilling to lend or because investors and shareholders choose not to commit further funds.

In either case of capital rationing, the company should expand its financial analysis to evaluate the Profitability Index, or PI, for each investment. The PI is equal to the present value of future cash flows (NPV plus initial investment amount) divided by the initial capital investment:

$$PI = \frac{\textit{Initial investment amount} + NPV_0}{\textit{Initial capital investment}}.$$

Let us assume that the company has three alternative investment projects at hand, Alternatives A, B, and C:

	Alternative A	Alternative B	Alternative C
NPV	€1,450,000	€950,000	€900,000
Initial investment amount	€5,000,000	€2,450,000	€2,400,000
PI	1.29	1.39	1.37

Judging solely on the basis of NPV, the company would choose Alternative A. However, if it employed capital rationing and we assumed an investment constraint of €5,000,000, the company should look at Alternatives B or C since both of their PIs are greater than Alternative A's. In fact, the company should undertake both Alternatives B and C because the combined €3,300,000 initial outlay is well below the limit and would increase NPV by €1,850,000 instead of €1,450,000 if Alternative A is chosen.

Differences in the investment alternatives' lifetimes may appear to make the analysis more complicated because the longer investment's results will not be available when the shorter investment ends. To investigate this apparent difficulty, however, we can always take the investment with the shorter lifetime and supplement it with a clean-cut financial investment at the market interest rate after its life has ended. This will give the two alternatives the same investment lifetime.

As an example, suppose we have two alternative investments, A and B, whose lifetimes consist of N and M periods, respectively, where N is shorter than M. Since A's lifetime is less than B's, to compare the investments properly we must first calculate the future value of Alternative A (i.e., $FV_{A,N}$). This is done, as usual, by compounding its net cash flows out to the end of Time N. Next, this amount, $FV_{A,N}$, is placed at the discount rate for M – N periods, which causes the amount to grow to $FV_{A,N} \cdot (1+R)^{M-N}$. In order to determine the total net present value of the project (i.e, Alternative A + financial investment), we then discount the final value back to Time 0, which yields the following equation:

$$NPV_{A,0} = FV_{A,N} \cdot (1+R)^{M-N} \cdot (1+R)^{-M} = FV_{A,N} \cdot (1+R)^{-N}.$$

From this equation we see that the financial investment does not impact the net present value at all. Accordingly, the NPV method is suitable for ranking alternative investments with different lifetimes.

This logic can be illustrated as shown in Figure 5.3 below:

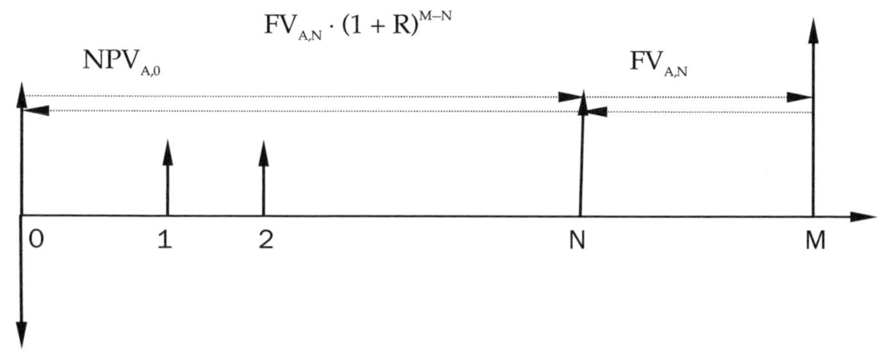

Figure 5.3 Real investment supplemented with a financial investment

Example 5.3
Suppose that the following three-year cash flow must be analyzed and compared with that for another project, which has a lifetime of five periods. For the analysis we assume a discount rate of 10 % per year.

Period	0	1	2	3	4	5
Alternative A	–€100,000	€75,000	€50,000	€25,000		

$NPV_{0,A} = -100{,}000 + 75{,}000 \cdot 1.1^{-1} + 50{,}000 \cdot 1.1^{-2} + 25{,}000 \cdot 1.1^{-3}.$

$NPV_{0,A} = €28{,}287.$

If we calculate Alternative A's future value at the end of the third period, we have:

$FV_{3,A} = -100{,}000 \cdot 1.1^{3} + 75{,}000 \cdot 1.1^{2} + 50{,}000 \cdot 1.1 + 25{,}000.$

$FV_{3,A} = €37{,}650.$

Compounding this amount at 10 % p.a. for another two periods to Time 5 yields:

$FV_{5,A} = 37{,}650 \cdot 1.1^{2} = €45{,}556.$

As a final step we calculate the present value of $FV_{5,A}$ by discounting the amount back to Time 0. This yields the following amount:

$NPV_{0,A} = 45{,}556 \cdot 1.1^{-5} = €28{,}287.$

This is exactly the same value we found above when calculating $NPV_{0,A}$ directly. Therefore we see that an investment placed at the market rate after its lifetime has ended will yield the same net present value as the one realized at the end of the initial investment period.

Example 5.4
By investing in energy-conserving equipment, a company will see a savings on its oil and electricity bills. Two alternative types of equipment are available:

1. Alternative A has an initial investment of €200,000 and is expected to provide annual savings of €80,000 over the next five years.
2. Alternative B is somewhat cheaper, having an initial investment of €150,000, but yielding annual savings of €75,000 over only four years.

Which of the two alternatives should the company choose if they are mutually exclusive and a discount rate of 10 % per year is applied?

Alternative A

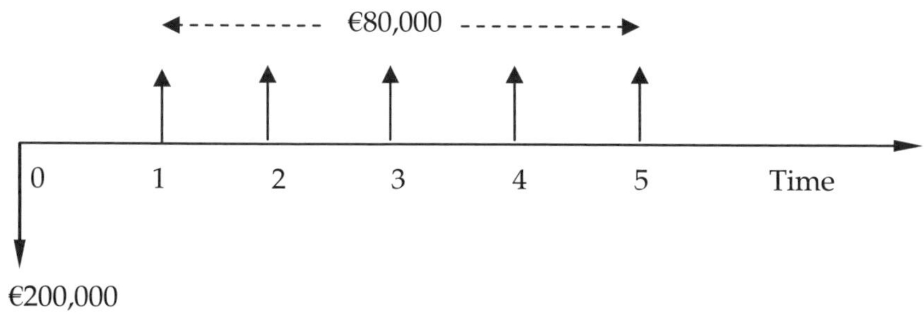

Alternative B

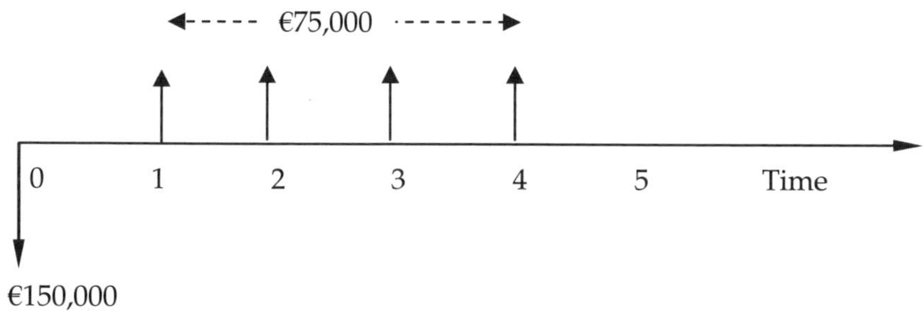

Alternative A: $NPV_0 = -200{,}000 + 80{,}000 \cdot PVIFA_{10\,\%,5} = €103{,}263.$

Alternative B: $NPV_0 = -150{,}000 + 75{,}000 \cdot PVIFA_{10\,\%,4} = €87{,}740.$

The company should choose Alternative A, as this yields the larger net present value of the two equipment types available.

Internal Rate of Return

Earlier, we concluded that a single investment is profitable if its internal rate of return exceeds the applied discount rate. When evaluating a number of alternative investment strategies, we would like to know, "*Among mutually exclusive investments, is the most profitable alternative the one with the highest internal rate of return?*".

Unfortunately, the answer is no. Three problems arise when using the internal rate of return to rank alternative projects:

1. The relative investment size of the given projects.
2. The lifetime of each project.
3. The discount rate cannot be taken into consideration.

When using the net present value method, the size of the investment is included directly in the calculation and we can eliminate the differences in lifetimes by supplementing the real investment with a financial investment at the discount rate without affecting the NPV. However, this is not the case with the internal rate of return. This will change, as can easily be seen through the following examples:

Example 5.5
A company's investment of €75,000 in labor-saving equipment will lead to an additional annual cash flow of €30,000 over the next five years, while an alternative type of equipment costing €100,000 will provide €37,500 per year over the same time frame. If we calculate the internal rate of return for each alternative, we have:

Alternative A: $0 = NPV_0 = -75{,}000 + 30{,}000 \cdot PVIFA_{IRR,\,5}.$

$\Rightarrow IRR = 28.7\ \%$ p.a.

Alternative B: $0 = NPV_0 = -100{,}000 + 37{,}500 \cdot PVIFA_{IRR,\,5}.$

$\Rightarrow IRR = 25.4\ \%$ p.a.

Both alternatives yield an internal rate of return which exceeds the 10 % p.a. discount rate we have used. Therefore, each investment is profitable in and of itself. We see that Alternative A has the highest internal rate of return. Therefore, this is the project which yields the highest return on invested capital at any point in time. If we select the absolute internal rate of return as our criteria for choosing the most profitable investment, we would choose Alternative A. Analyzing the situation more closely; we see that Alternative A has "only" €75,000 invested, whereas the sum for Alternative B is €100,000. Alternative A returns 28.7 % per year on invested capital vs. 25.4 % per year on invested capital for Alternative B. However, even though Alternative B yields 3.3 % less per year, we are investing a larger amount. If we had used the net present value method with a discount rate of 10 % per year, we would have:

Alternative A: $NPV_0 = -75{,}000 + 30{,}000 \cdot PVIFA_{10\,\%,\,5} = €38{,}724.$

Alternative B: $NPV_0 = -100{,}000 + 37{,}500 \cdot PVIFA_{10\,\%,\,5} = €42{,}155.$

Clearly Alternative B has the larger net present value and is therefore the optimal choice, even though its IRR is lower than Alternative A's.

From the calculations above, we see that the absolute internal rate of return method and the NPV method can lead to different rankings of project profitability.

In summary, when alternative investment strategies involve different amounts of money, comparing the projects based only on the internal rate of return may lead to erroneous conclusions because investor value creation is also dependent upon the amount invested.

Example 5.6
Two mutually exclusive investments require an initial investment of €100,000. Alternative A is estimated to return an annual positive cash flow of €35,500 over the next four years. Meanwhile, Alternative B is estimated to return an annual positive cash flow of €35,000 over the next five years. Which of the two investments should we choose?

If we calculate the internal rate of return for both alternatives, we have:

Alternative A: $0 = NPV_0 = -100{,}000 + 35{,}500 \cdot PVIFA_{IRR,\,4}.$

$\Rightarrow IRR = 15.67\ \%$ p.a.

Alternative B: $0 = NPV_0 = -100{,}000 + 30{,}000 \cdot PVIFA_{IRR,\,5}.$
$\Rightarrow IRR = 15.24\ \%$ p.a.

Based on their internal rates of return, both alternatives are profitable if we assume an applied discount rate of 10 % per year. We see that Alternative A yields a slightly higher internal rate of return than Alternative B, but on the other hand we receive the return on investment in Alternative B for an additional year

Now let us calculate the net present value for each alternative using a discount rate of 10 % per year:

Alternative A: $NPV_0 = -100{,}000 + 35{,}500 \cdot PVIFA_{10\,\%,4} = €12{,}530.$

Alternative B: $NPV_0 = -100{,}000 + 30{,}000 \cdot PVIFA_{10\,\%,5} = €13{,}724.$

Again, we see that the absolute internal rate of return method and the NPV method rank the attractiveness of the investment alternatives differently. Hence, even when we are comparing projects with the same investment amounts, we can make a decision based solely on internal rate of return only if: 1) the investment lifetime of the most attractive investment is greater than or equal to that of the less attractive investment alternative, and if 2) the internal rate of return is higher than the applied investor discount rate.

We have seen in Examples 5.5 and 5.6 that the less attractive investment alternative can actually yield the higher internal rate of return because this method does not correctly consider the invested amounts or investment lifetimes. Therefore, the absolute internal rate of return *cannot* be used as criteria for ranking the profitability of alternative investments.

However, this problem can be handled through a structured approach: If the investment projects are ranked according to their internal rates of return, where the investment with the highest IRR is ranked first, the investment with the next highest IRR is ranked second, and so on, then the following types projects can be excluded beforehand:

Those with:

1. Lower or similar internal rates of return.
2. Smaller or similar initial investments.
3. Shorter or similar lifetimes.

After eliminating as many projects as possible, we can compare those which remain by analyzing the differences in cash flow as we move from one to the next. Using the data from Example 5.5 to illustrate this procedure, we have:

Period	**0**	**1**	**2**	**3**	**4**	**5**
Alternative A	–€75,000	€30,000	€30,000	€30,000	€30,000	€30,000
Change from A to B	–€25,000	€7,500	€7,500	€7,500	€7,500	€7,500

At this point we define the cash flow difference from opting for Alternative B rather than Alternative 1 as an investment possibility in itself which is called "Change from A to B". This investment of €25,000 in Time 0 will yield an incremental positive cash flow of €7,500 in each of the following five years vs. Alternative A. When we calculate the internal rate of return and net present value for this "difference investment", we have:

$$NPV_0 = -25{,}000 + 7{,}500 \cdot PVIFA_{10\,\%,\,5} = €3{,}431.$$

$$0 = NPV_0 = -25{,}000 + 7{,}500 \cdot PVIFA_{IRR,\,5} \Rightarrow IRR = 15.24\ \%\ \text{p.a.}$$

From this, we see that both the NPV and IRR methods indicate that we should choose Alternative B over Alternative A because the net present value is positive and the IRR is higher than the 10 % discount rate applied. Proceeding similarly with the numbers from Example 5.6, we get:

Period	**0**	**1**	**2**	**3**	**4**	**5**
Alternative A	–€100,000	€35,500	€35,500	€35,500	€35,500	
Change from A to B	0	–€5,500	–€5,500	–€5,500	–€5,500	€30,000

Here, choosing investment Alternative 2 instead of Alternative A would mean relinquishing €5,500 in each of the first four years but receiving €30,000 in the fifth year. If we calculate the NPV and IRR of this decision, we have:

$$NPV_0 = -5{,}500 \cdot PVIFA_{10\,\%,\,4} + 30{,}000 \cdot (1 + 0.1)^{-5} = €1{,}193.$$

$$0 = NPV_0 = -5{,}500 \cdot PVIFA_{IRR,\,4} + 30{,}000 \cdot (1 + IRR)^{-5} \Rightarrow IRR = 12.80\ \%\ \text{p.a.}$$

Once again, the NPV and IRR methods yield the same result: The difference investment is profitable, so we should switch from Alternative A to Alternative B.

Based on the examples above, we conclude that the absolute internal rate of return method does not always lead to a proper ranking of alternative investment projects. However, we can overcome this deficiency by finding the difference in cash flows and calculating the internal rate of return on this newly derived cash flow. It should be noted, though, that this method can be applied only in situations where the differential cash flow has but one sign change.

Before closing the discussion on the IRR Method, there is one very important area of investments to mention where the absolute internal rate of return is used as a determining criteria – that of pure financial investments. Financial investments are often quite flexible with regard to the investment's size and time horizon. For example, if we wanted to buy bonds, the investment amount could be almost freely fixed and the bonds resold at any time. This is why companies with excess liquidity over a specified time frame often choose to proceed with a financial investment such as buying bonds, placing money in a fixed-term deposit account, or the like. When making such investments, the absolute internal rate of return method is often used as the main criteria for ranking these investments' profitability.

The Annuity

We have seen that the NPV method can be directly applied when ranking alternative projects, even if the investment alternatives involve different amounts and lifetimes. The internal rate of return can also do this, though in a somewhat more complicated fashion. Now we turn the annuity method. Will it give a correct ranking of the alternative investments, or will difficulties arise? In order to answer this question, we must first distinguish between two types of situations:

1. All investment alternatives have similar lifetimes.
2. All investment alternatives have different lifetimes.

If all investment alternatives have similar lifetimes, the annuities will be directly comparable and this method will be suitable for ranking the respective alternatives.

As we have seen earlier, the net present value method will always provide the correct ranking for any set of investment alternatives. The relationship between the net present value and the annuity, as given in Chapter 2 and repeated here, is defined as follows:

$$NPV_0 = A \cdot PVIFA_{I,N}.$$

If the lifetime *N* and interest rate *i* are similar for all the investment alternatives at hand, then the factor $PVIFA_{I,N}$ becomes a constant. This results in a direct proportionality between the projects' NPV_0 and their calculated annuities, which makes the investments comparable.

However, if the projects do not have similar lifetimes a direct proportionality between each investment's NPV_0 and annuity no longer exists because *N* is not the same for all projects. Hence, the factor $PVIFA_{I,N}$ will be different for each investment. This means we cannot be certain that the annuity (once calculated from project's lifetime) will be valid for ranking the various alternative investments. It follows logically from this that annuities cannot meaningfully be compared in this case.

Example 5.7

The choice between two alternative projects results in separate annuities. Alternative A has an annuity of €60,000 per period for five periods, while Alternative B's annuity yields €50,000 over seven periods. Which of the two alternatives should we choose?

The solution to this question depends on our time preference and, consequently, the discount rate applied. If we prefer a relatively fast return (as reflected in a high discount rate), we would probably opt for €60,000 per period over five periods instead of €50,000 for each of seven periods. On the other hand, if we have time to wait (as a lower discount rate would imply), we might prefer €50,000 per period for seven periods over €60,000 for five.

Alternative A

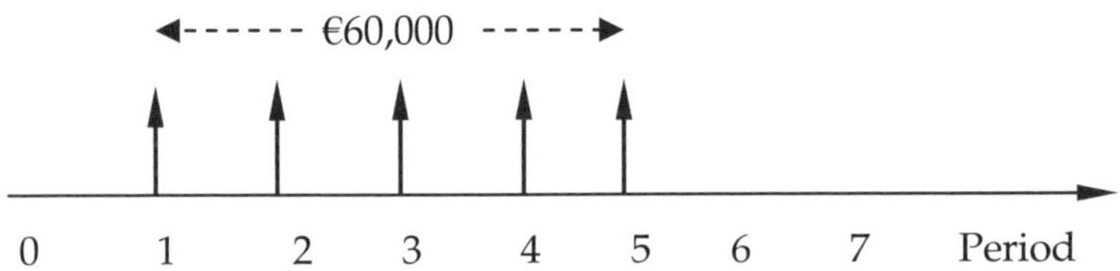

Alternative B

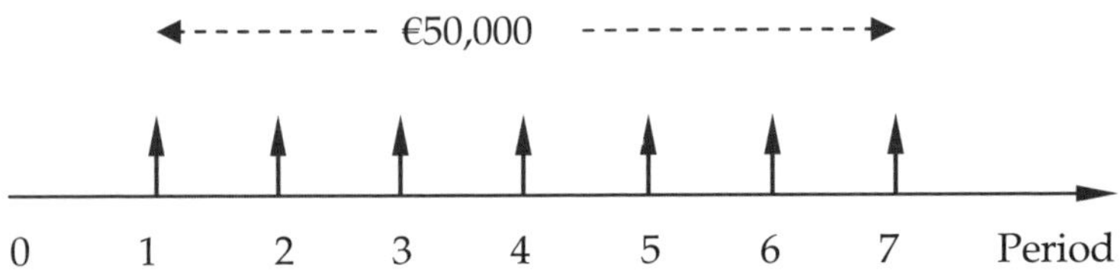

If we assume a 10 % discount rate, which reflects a relatively patient, long-term investor, we obtain the following results:

Alternative A: $NPV_0 = 60{,}000 \cdot PVIFA_{10\,\%,\,5} =$ €227,447.

Alternative B: $NPV_0 = 50{,}000 \cdot PVIFA_{10\,\%,\,7} =$ €243,421.

Therefore, at a discount rate of 10 % per year, we would prefer Alternative B because its net present value is higher than that of Alternative A. However, if the discount rate is changed to 30 % per year, which likely indicates a short-term investor with a rapid payback preference, the picture changes as follows:

Alternative A: $NPV_0 = 60{,}000 \cdot PVIFA_{30\,\%,5} =$ €146,134.

Alternative B: $NPV_0 = 50{,}000 \cdot PVIFA_{30\,\%,7} =$ €140,106.

Now Alternative A has become the more attractive investment. From this we see that the annuity method does not always yield the correct profitability ranking for projects with varying lifetimes. Only if the lifetimes of the alternative investments are equal can the annuity method be applied.

From a series of mutually exclusive alternative investments with similar lifetimes, the most profitable investment is the one having the highest annuity

The following two tables summarize how to evaluate alternative investments with similar lifetimes and different lifetimes respectively:

Alternative investments with similar lifetimes

	Net Present Value	**Relative Internal Rate of return**	**Annuity**
Applicability	Always	Difficult to apply	Always
Decision criteria	Highest NPV	Continue as long as the difference investment yields an internal rate of return larger than the discount rate	Largest annuity

Alternative investments with different lifetimes

	Net Present Value	Relative Internal Rate of return	Annuity
Applicability	Always	Difficult to apply	Not applicable
Decision criteria	Highest NPV	Continue as long as the difference investment yields an internal rate of return larger than the discount rate	None

The Payback Method

The final investment measure we will consider in this chapter is known as the payback method. It is widely used in practice because it provides a benchmark for evaluating an investment project's liquidity. However, it has a number of inadequacies from a theoretical perspective since it does not give the full view needed for evaluating individual projects and is unsuitable for evaluating alternative investments.

The payback method works by accumulating the cash flows from each period, then determining the period the accumulated cash flow turns positive. This is known as the break-even point and it occurs, when cash outflows have been balanced by an equal amount of cash inflows.

The key weaknesses of this method are as follows:

1. Cash flows expected late in the period receive an equal weighting to those expected early if no discounting is made.
2. Cash flows after the payback period are ignored.
3. The threshold payback period is subjectively determined.

The first weakness can be mitigated by accumulating the discounted net cash flows at each point in time, rather than using the aggregate cash flow corresponding to each period. Even if this extra step is taken, however, the last two weaknesses remain valid.

The wide popularity and usage of the payback method is easy to understand; after all, it is very simple to use and tells us when the investment has paid itself off. This can be helpful information when analyzing long-lived, relatively risky investment strategies because the net cash flows' uncertainty will increase the farther into the future we go.

If the payback period is reasonably short and we have a reliable expectation of cash flows, it could be argued that we have a criterion for at least evaluating whether the investment alternative is attractive in itself. Any positive cash flow received after the payback period could be considered an added benefit because even if they never actually materialized, we still would have realized a return on our investment up until the break-even point was reached. The main drawback, however, is that this still says nothing about the investment's attractiveness.

Example 5.8
A certain manufacturing company has the opportunity to purchase some new machinery for a cost of €200,000. The machinery has an anticipated useful life of six years and is expected to generate annual cost savings through the efficiency improvements it provides. The investment project's cash flows are given in the table below:

Period	**0**	**1**	**2**	**3**	**4**	**5**	**6**
	–€200,000	€40,000	€60,000	€80,000	€80,000	€60,000	€60,000

Applying a discount rate of 10 % per year would provide the accumulated discounted and non-discounted cash flows as illustrated in Figure 5.4:

Period	**0**	**1**	**2**	**3**	**4**	**5**	**6**
	–€200,000	–€160,000	–€10,000	–€20,000	€60,000	€120,000	€160,000
	–€200,000	–€163,636	–€114,050	–€53,944	€696	€37,952	€60,530

Figure 5.4 Accumulated cash flow as a function of time

As the graph illustrates, the payback period is roughly 3.25 years when looking at the non-discounted cash flow, but it increases to nearly four years when the discounted cash flow is used.

If the company had defined four years as the maximum length of time to recoup the initial capital expenditure, the investment would be acceptable because the estimated actual payback would occur prior to the specified time frame's completion. However, if the maximum payback time had been set at three years, the investment would not be considered attractive.

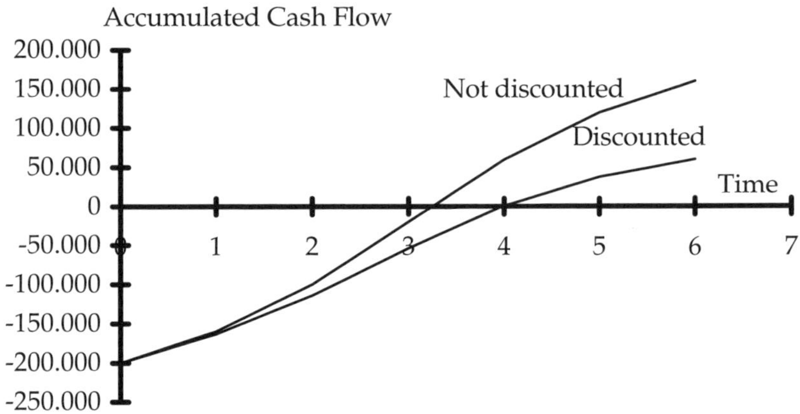

Figure 5.4 Accumulated cash flow as a function of time

As we conclude this chapter, we can summarize the four best methods for evaluating various investments as follows:

	Net Present Value	Absolute Internal Rate of Return	Relative Internal Rate of Return	Annuity
Individual Investment	+	+		+
Alternative Investments				
Similar Lifetime	+		+	+
Different Lifetime	+			

CHAPTER 6

Tax and Inflation

Tax and Cash Flow

Tax legislation is typically very comprehensive and complicated, so a detailed review and calculation of corporate taxes usually requires the involvement and advice of tax specialists. In this chapter we will be content to look at the main principles and fundamental effects of tax payments as they relate to investment projects.

The main principles of tax payment are defined as:

1. All income is taxed.
2. All costs are tax-deductible.

In tax situations, the terms *income* and *costs* mark a difference in terminology compared to the investment analysis. This is because tax calculations are generally based on the accounting period's income and cost, whereas the investment analysis considers cash flows.
The implication is that:

> The period's income and cost influence the cash flow through tax payments.

After-tax cash flow is thus comprised of all the period's cash flows minus tax payments resulting from the period's income and cost.

The applied discount rate for investment analysis must correspond to the investment cash flow. This means that a before-tax investment analysis of cash flows must use the before-tax discount rate, and an after-tax investment analysis must use the after-tax discount rate. So, we now have two types of discount rates: a discount rate before tax, and a discount rate for afterwards:

Discount rate after tax = Discount rate before tax · (1 – tax rate).

To establish an investment's after-tax cash flow, we must first consider which specific tax rules are applicable for the project's actual incomes and costs. As mentioned earlier, the basic principles are that all income is taxed and that all costs are tax-deductible:

Types of taxable income:

1. Sales income.
2. Interest/financial income.
3. Capital gains, which occur when an asset is sold for more than its book value.

Tax-deductible costs:

1. Fixed and variable costs.
2. Interest/financial expenses.
3. Depreciation.
4. Capital losses, which occur when an asset is sold for less than its book value.

Deduction of interest/financial expenses is handled implicitly by adjusting the discount rate to an after-tax discount rate.

Tax legislation is much more complicated than the points described in brief above. One reason is that taxes are often subject to exceptions and special rules because governments use them as an instrument to promote or inhibit certain economic activities. Also, the legislation governing depreciation typically varies for different types of equipment and facilities, resulting in other sets of rules. For our purposes of investment analysis, however, we will use the above framework.

Having defined cash flow and the discount rate on both a before-tax and an after-tax basis, it is important to be consistent in our use of them. The following simple relationship applies:

Cash flow	Discount rate
Before-tax cash flow *None* of the tax-induced consequences such as tax payments/tax deductions are included in the cash flow	Before-tax discount rate: I_{nom}
After-tax cash flow *All* of the tax-induced consequences are included in the cash flow	After-tax discount rate: $I_{after\ tax} = I_{nom} \cdot (1\text{- tax rate})$

The General Procedure for Handling of Tax

The following systematic approach can be applied to investment analysis on an after-tax basis:

1. Establish cash flow before tax.
2. Calculate the net taxable income/loss (i.e. tax base).
3. Calculate tax.
4. Establish cash flow after tax.

Establish cash flow before tax
The first step is to establish the investment's before-tax cash flow in accordance with the principles already discussed. This is done by analyzing capital expenditures, financing, sales, costs, and assumptions.

	0	**1**			**N**
Investment					
Cash inflow					
Cash outflow					
Changes to working capital					
Cash flow before tax					

Calculate the net taxable income/loss (tax base)

The net taxable income/loss (tax base) is calculated by subtracting all tax deductible costs and depreciation from gross taxable income.

	0	1			N
Gross taxable income					
Tax deductible costs					
Depreciation					
Other taxable income or costs					
Net taxable income/loss (tax base)					

Calculate tax

The expected tax is calculated by multiplying net taxable income/loss (tax base) by the tax rate. The tax payment can be positive or negative, depending on the tax base. A negative tax payment (taxable loss) can typically be carried forward to future years to offset positive tax payments (taxable income).

	0	1			N
Net taxable income/loss (tax base)					
Tax rate					
Tax payment					

Establish cash flow after tax

The after-tax cash flow is established by subtracting calculated tax payments from the before-tax cash flow.

	0	1			N
Before tax cash flow					
Tax payment					
After tax cash flow					

Example 6.1

A firm is considering whether to invest €100,000 in a new production facility. The facility will increase the firm's cash flow profits by €40,000 in the first year, but afterwards they are expected to decrease by €2,000 per year. The cost of operation, repair and maintenance amount to €6,175 in the first year and will rise by 30 % per year. The facility's lifespan is estimated at 7 years, after which it will be sold at book value. The firm uses a before-tax discount rate of 12 % p.a. The provisions for depreciation are made per the balance method at 30 % p.a. Finally, the firm expects a tax rate of 34 % over the next seven years.

First, the investment is analyzed without considering tax effects:

Year t	0	1	2	3	4	5	6	7
Investment	–100,000							
Contribution margin		40,000	38,000	36,000	34,000	32,000	30,000	28,000
Operational cost		–6,175	–8,028	–10,436	–13,566	–17,636	–22,927	–29,806
Scrap value								8,235
Cash flow	–100.000	33,825	29,973	25,564	20,434	14,364	7,073	6,430

We can now calculate the net present value, internal rate of return and annuity of this individual investment, with the following results:

Net present value, NPV_0: = – €81
The internal rate of return: = 11.97 % p.a.
Annuity: = –€18 per year

We see that the project is not attractive when evaluated on a before-tax basis. The net present value and annuity are both negative, and the internal rate of return is slightly less than the discount rate.

We will now include tax factors in the investment analysis. We will start by first calculating the cash flow before tax, then subtracting tax payments.

The amount invested in Year 0 does not have tax implications. The same is true for the investment's terminal value in Year 7 since it is assumed that the facility is sold at book value. The profit contribution for each year will result in a tax payment, while the operating cost results in a tax deduction. And finally, the production facility will experience depreciation, which results in a tax deduction.

Year t	0	1	2	3	4	5	6	7
Contribution margin		40,000	38,000	36,000	34,000	32,000	30,000	28,000
Operational cost		–6,175	–8,028	–10,436	–13,566	–17,636	–22,927	–29,806
Depreciation		–30,000	–21,000	–14,700	–10,290	–7,203	–5,042	–3,529
Tax basis		3,825	8,973	10,864	10,144	7,161	2,031	–5,335
Tax 34 %		1,301	3,051	3,694	3,449	2,435	690	–1,814
Cash flow before tax	–100.000	33,825	29,973	25,564	20,434	14,364	7,073	6,430
Tax		1,301	3,051	3,694	3,449	2,435	690	–1,814
Cash flow after tax	–100,000	32,525	26,922	21,870	16,985	11,929	6,382	8,244

To be consistent, we apply the after tax discount rate which is calculated as: 12 % · (1 – 0.34) = 7.9 % p.a. Again, using the three fundamental metrics for assessment of a single investment's benefit we have:

Net present value, NPV_0	= €198
The internal rate of return, IRR	= 8.0 % p.a.
Annuity	= €38 per year

The project thus becomes slightly positive when the firm takes tax factors into consideration. The net present value and the annuity are both positive. The internal rate of return is 8 % p.a., slightly larger than the 7.9 % after-tax discount rate.

The reason the project becomes positive when tax factors are considered is because the largest depreciation amounts (and thus the largest tax deductions) occur in the early years of the project. All else being equal, maximizing after-tax cash flows in the first years of the project leads to a higher net present value.

Example 6.2
Smith's Metal Goods is a larger producer of hardware and accessories and has always considered itself a well-positioned metal goods firm with a skilled workforce. Lately, however, production technology has been advancing and the company feels it may be at risk of falling behind competitors. Many of these have already changed to newer technology, which results in the following range of benefits and savings:

1. Raw materials can be used more efficiently, which minimizes waste.
2. The time needed for start-up and switching between products is less. This allows smaller batch sizes, which reduces stocks of raw materials and semi-finished products.
3. Less space is required for production and storage.

This ability to produce at lower cost is putting pressure on the industry, and Smith's feels that it must invest in technology in order to remain competitive. Chief executive John Smith, as the family-owned company's third-generation leader, is considering purchasing new equipment for some of the firm's production lines.

The production lines under consideration for investment run independently of the remaining production and can thus be analyzed separately. The existing production equipment in that area was purchased four years ago at a cost of €1,600,000. Smith's uses a 30 % per year balance depreciation on all its production equipment. The equipment is presently valued at €500,000 and has been well-maintained. It is estimated to have a realistic lifespan of at least seven more years, after which it could be sold for €100,000.

The new equipment that Smith's Metal Goods is considering costs €1,250,000 and has an expected lifespan of seven years. After that, it would be worth €50,000 at most.

The financial impact of changing to newer technology is as follows:

1. The firm would save €40,000 annually in raw materials.
2. The money tied up in raw material stocks would decrease from €100,000 to €30,000.
3. The space required for storage and production would be reduced by 500 sq. ft. For costing purposes, Smith's value floor space at €350 per sq. ft. (all-inclusive rent equivalent).

The easiest way to analyze this project is to look at the incremental cash flow changes which the investment in new technology will provide over the next seven years. The reduction in money tied up in raw material stocks will be included, as well as the reduction in storage costs and the value of improved floor space utilization.

It is debatable whether or not the value of floor space saved should be included in the investment calculation. It depends on whether the space to be freed up has an alternative use which can generate extra revenue for the company. In the situation at hand, all floor space is used for storage and production and there are plans to expand the factory in approximately two years. Consequently, it is fair to include the floor space savings in the investment calculation. This is done by multiplying the *average rent per square foot by the number of square feet made available.*

The investment required for the new equipment is €1,250,000. But, since the existing equipment can be sold for €500,000 the net investment is the difference of €750,000. On the negative, in seven years the existing equipment could be sold for €100,000, whereas the new equipment will bring only €50,000. On an incremental basis, then, the equipment cash flow in Year 7 would be reduced by €50,000.

The reduction in required storage capacity frees up €70,000 immediately (€100,000 - €30,000) as raw material stock can be reduced from €100,000 to €30,000. This in turn means that in seven years' time only €30,000 will be freed up, as raw material stocks at that time will naturally only amount to the reduced €30,000. At that time, the storage with the existing production equipment would have been worth €100,000 if the reduction has not been made.

The reduction in floor space equates to a yearly savings of €175,000 (€350 · 500 s.f.).

Experience tells John Smith that capital commitments for similar projects have earned an average of 13 % p.a. before taxes, so this is the applied discount rate to use.

Cash flow on a before-tax basis is therefore calculated as follows:

Year (€1,000)	0	1	2	3	4	5	6	7
Change in investment	–750							–50
Change in storage	70							
Raw material savings		40	40	40	40	40	40	40
Freeing of space		175	175	175	175	175	175	175
Cash flow before tax	–680	215	215	215	215	215	215	95

We can now calculate the net present value, internal rate of return and annuity on a before-tax basis:

Net present value, NPV_0 = €219,854
The internal rate of return, IRR = 23.4 % p.a.
Annuity = €49,711 per year

The project is profitable before tax is considered.

It should be noted that the project is only profitable when the value of the floor space savings is included. Saved rent amounts to €175,000 per year, and the investment annuity is about €50,000 per year. In other words, if the saved rent is eliminated, the project will yield a net loss of approximately €125,000 per year.

When we take tax into consideration, we calculate the changes caused by tax payments. The old equipment has been depreciated over several years and now has a book value of €384,160. This amount is the basis of future depreciation if no investments are made in new equipment. If new equipment is purchased, the depreciation basis will be the investment cost, €1,250,000. In this case the old equipment can be sold for €500,000. With a book value of €384,160, there will be a capital gain of €115,840. This is subject to tax.

If Smith's Metal Goods were to keep its old equipment an additional seven years, its book value would decrease to €31,637. When sold at the end of Year 7 for €100,000, there would be a capital gain of €68,363 (€100,000 - €31,637).

If new equipment is purchased and sees a 30 % per year balance depreciation, it will have a book value of €102,943 at the end of its seven-year life. With an expected selling price of €50,000, this implies a capital loss of €52,943 (€50,000 - €102,943).

The net result is an overall incremental decrease of €121,306 in the Year 7 tax base (€68,363 + €52,943) as the €68,363 capital gain from keeping the existing equipment is avoided and the company instead incurring a €52,943 capital loss from the purchase of the new equipment.

Also, as we saw previously, there is an increased cash flow of €215,000 per year from the reduction in raw materials and floor space rent.

We can now calculate the combined change in the tax base from depreciation and capital gains.

Year (€1,000)	**0**	**1**	**2**	**3**	**4**	**5**	**6**	**7**
Budgeted depreciation on existing equipment		115	81	56	40	28	19	14
Budgeted depreciation on new equipment		375	263	184	129	90	63	44
Change in depreciation from existing to new equipment		260	182	127	89	62	44	31
Change in capital gain/loss	116							–121
Total change in depreciation and capital gain/loss	116	260	182	127	89	62	44	–90

We can combine these changes in depreciation and capital gains/losses with the cash flow from savings in raw materials and from freeing up of space, in order to calculate the tax basis and the tax payments, assuming a tax rate of 34 %:

Year (€1,000)	**0**	**1**	**2**	**3**	**4**	**5**	**6**	**7**
Raw material savings		40	40	40	40	40	40	40
Freeing up of space		175	175	175	175	175	175	175
Total change in depreciation and capital gain/loss (from above)	116	260	182	127	89	62	44	–90
Tax base	116	-45	33	88	126	153	171	63
Tax (34 %)	39	-15	11	30	43	52	58	21

Since we know the expected tax payments every year, we can now calculate the after-tax cash flows from those already determined on a before-tax basis above:

Year (€1,000)	0	1	2	3	4	5	6	7
Cash flow before tax	–680	215	215	215	215	215	215	95
Cash flow after tax	–719	230	204	185	172	163	157	74

Based on these assumptions, the after-tax cash flows can be used to analyze the investment strategy. With a tax rate of 34 %, the discount rate is 8.6 % p.a. This gives the following results:

Net present value, NPV_0	= €179,025
The internal rate of return, IRR	= 16.7 % p.a.
Annuity	= €35,071 per year

The investment is profitable on an after-tax basis, under the assumption that freed-up floor space has an alternative use worth €175,000 per year.

With a tax rate of 34 %, the NPV difference in the investment analysis on a before- and after-tax basis is not significant (€219,854 vs. €179,025). Consequently, we see that after-tax calculations are mostly relevant for large, complicated investment strategies. In smaller and more straightforward investment projects, the marginal effect of taking tax issues into account may be limited, especially when considering the uncertainties linked to all other variables involved in an investment analysis. Also, future tax payments are liable to regulatory changes and cannot be seen in isolation from the company's overall tax situation.

Inflation and Cash Flow

The price of goods and services changes over time. Historically, the trend is upwards. Yet all prices do not rise at the same rate, and some may actually decrease. To assess the combined effect of an economy's price increases or decreases, we define a basket of relevant goods and services, assigning a weight to each one. To reach a common denominator we multiply the price variation in each good and service by the weight which each one carries, then tabulate the result. This provides a number which we define as the economy's *inflation*. It reflects the overall change in price from one year to the next for the basket of goods and services.

Inflation is calculated as the percentage change in the total price for a defined basket of goods and services from one point in time to another.

The development of inflation in the case of Denmark since 1915, calculated on the basis of the consumer price index is shown in Figure 6.1.

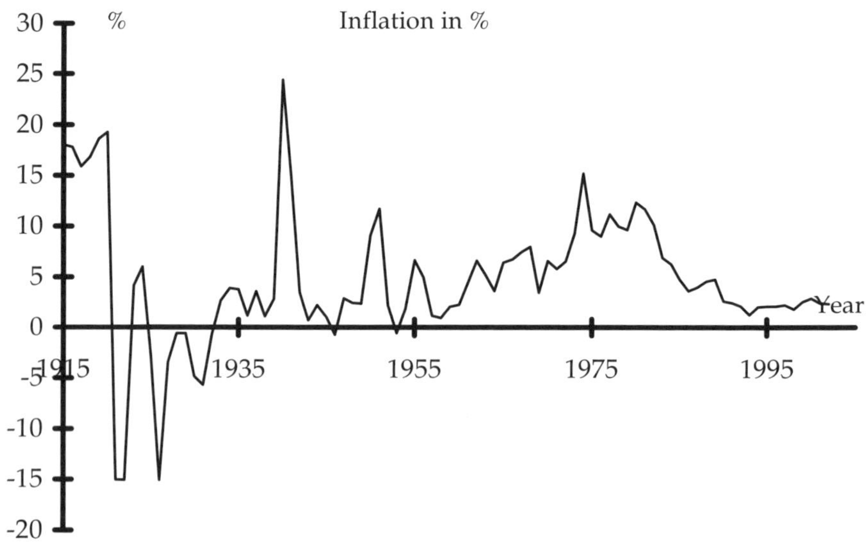

Figure 6.1 Development of inflation in Denmark 1915-2002

Comments:

Calculated on the basis of the following:

1. Period 1814-1980: Hans Chr. Johansen: Dansk historisk statistik, 1814-1980, Gyldendal, 1984. Table 8.1. Price index 1815-1980; consumer price index.
2. Period 1981-2002: Danmarks statistik: Statistisk tiårsoversigt.

The graph illustrates the significant variation in inflation over time and in different economic regions. In some situations prices can decrease. This is called deflation.

The handling of inflation is important in investment analysis, and we must be consistent about whether inflation is included in our calculations or not. For example, let us assume that a company can purchase 100 units of a product today for a total price of €10,000. This is an average price of €100 per product unit. If the purchase is postponed by a year, the €10,000 will earn an interest rate of perhaps 10 %. This means that the €10,000 will have increased to €11,000 within a year. During the year the inflation is assumed to be 3 %. Within that year the average price will have risen to €103. Therefore, one year from now the company will be able to purchase $\frac{11{,}000}{103} = 106.8$ product units, compared to 100 product units right now. The real rate of return, measured in purchasing power, is thus calculated to be: $\frac{106.8 - 100}{100} = 0.068$ or 6.8 %.

We can speak of a *financial interest rate* and a *purchasing power interest rate.* In this case they are 10 % p.a. and 6.8 % p.a., respectively. We traditionally call these two interest rates as follows:

> *Nominal interest rate* - the rate of return, or interest, measured in money. This is also known as the *nominal price.*
>
> *Real interest rate* - the rate of return, or interest, measured in purchasing power. This is also known as the *real price.*

The relationship between the inflation, nominal interest rate, and real interest rate can be clearly established and put into a formula. If we define the following abbreviations:

R_{nom}	for the nominal interest rate.
R_{real}	for the real interest rate.
q	for the inflation.

The following relationship applies:

$$(1 + I_{nom}) = (1 + I_{real}) \cdot (1 + q) .$$

Hence we have:

$$I_{real} = \frac{1 + I_{nom}}{1 + q} - 1 \quad \text{or} \quad I_{real} = \frac{I_{nom} - q}{1 + q}.$$

We can now calculate the real interest rate if we know the nominal interest rate and the inflation.

Figure 6.2 below shows the development of the effective interest rate for Danish mortgage credit bonds at the end of the year.

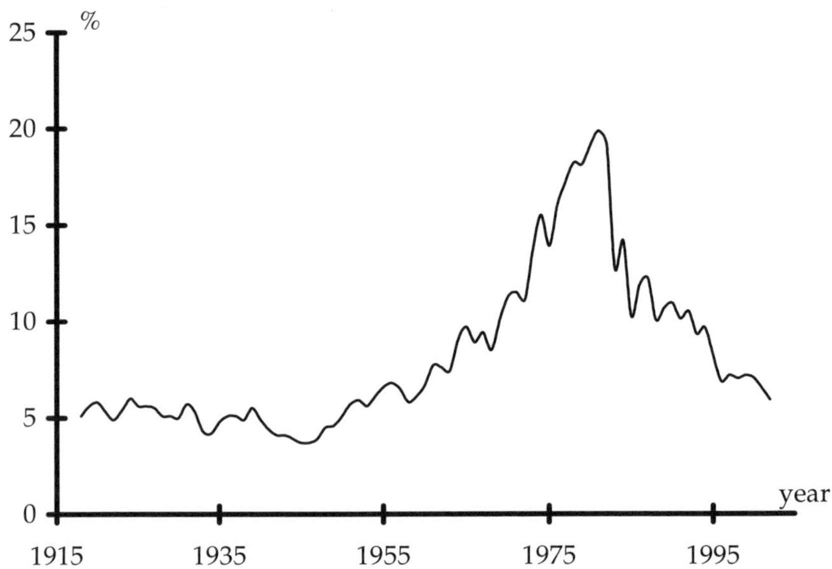

Figure 6.2 Development of the effective Danish bond interest rate 1915-2002

Sources:

1. Period 1814-1980: Hans Chr. Johansen: Dansk historisk statistik, 1814-1980, Gyldendal, 1984. Table 6.9. Rate of interests 1814-1980. Effective rate of return of the mortgage credit bond.
2. Period 1981-2002: Danmarks statistik: Statistisk tiårsoversigt.

If the effective bond interest rate is used as an expression for the market interest rate, the real interest rate can be estimated by subtracting the inflation from the market interest rate. The result is shown in Figure 6.3. This shows that over this time there have been brief periods with a negative real interest rate. It also appears that the real interest rate has been relatively stable over the past 25 years, varying only between 5.5 % and 7.5 % p.a. It may further be said that the real interest rate has been falling for the past several years.

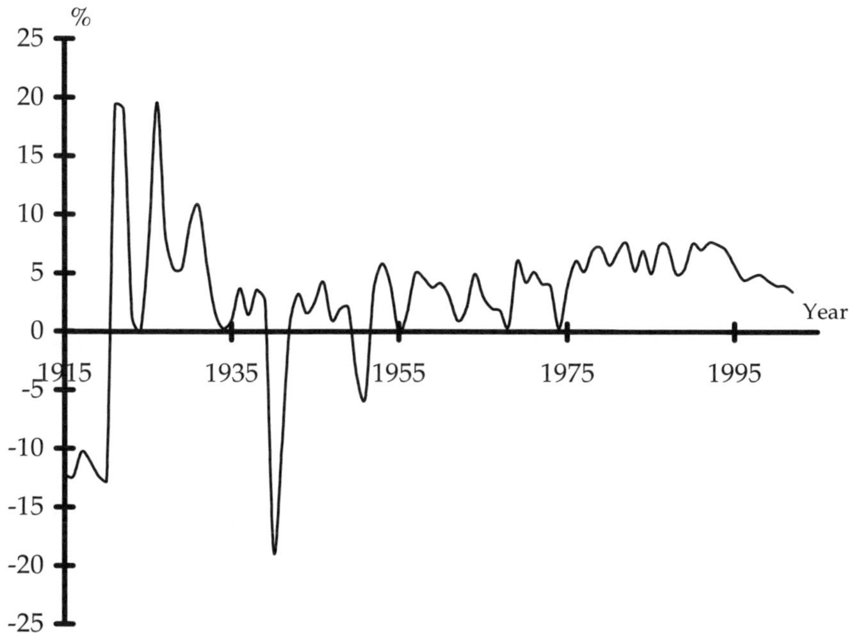

Figure 6.3 Development of the real interest rate in Denmark 1915-2002

The uncertainty related to forecasting future inflation and the real interest rate obviously complicates the determination of what discount rate to apply when performing investment analysis, especially for projects with a lengthy time horizon.

In investment analysis there is no rule as to whether future cash flows should be stated in nominal or real prices. Therefore it is paramount that we have a clear understanding as to which principle was used to develop our data and how it is to be interpreted. Similarly, for our calculations to be correct it is important that the applied discount rate correspond to the cash flow.

Some rules of thumb apply:

1. *The cash flow data for real investments will often be given in real prices.* This is due to the fact that the basis for real investments is often expressed in quantities, i.e. number of units produced, raw material volumes consumed, time required for each unit produced, etc. *Under the assumption that prices follow the general inflation trend, it will typically be easiest to develop a volume projection and then multiply by existing prices.*
2. *The cash flow data for financial investments will often be given in nominal prices.* This is because financial investments typically involve the buying and selling of claims, bonds, mortgages, loans, etc. *Future cash flows will typically be calculated and written into a loan document or similar agreement. These are nominal prices, even though the numbers themselves are often constant.*

Exceptions do exist, especially with real investments. Some future cash flows may be stated in nominal prices; others in real prices or even in mixed prices. Overall, it is an individual decision whether to state the cash flow in real or nominal prices. The essential thing is that all cash flows be classified the same (in either real or nominal prices) and that the applied discount rate match the category which has been selected. Consequently, if the investment analysis' data contains cash flows in both real and nominal prices, a decision must be made which category to apply. Then all cash flows in the other category must be converted to the one selected.

Net Present Value

We will calculate the investment's net present value using both real and nominal prices. This will show that the result is identical regardless of the data used. Let CF_t represent cash flow at time *t* in nominal prices. I_{nom}, I_{real}, and q are used for the nominal interest rate, the real interest rate and the inflation, respectively, and all are assumed to be constant throughout the project's life. The net present value in nominal prices is:

$$NPV_0 = \sum_{t=0}^{N} CF_t \cdot (1+I_{nom})^{-t}.$$

Cash flow in real prices can be calculated as:

CF_t in nominal prices = CF_t in real prices $\cdot (1 + q)^t$

and

$$(1 + I_{nom}) = (1 + I_{real}) \cdot (1 + q).$$

NPV_0 can then be written as:

$$NPV_0 = \sum_{t=0}^{N} CF_t \text{ in real prices } \cdot (1+q)^t \cdot (1+I_{real})^{-t} \cdot (1+q)^{-t},$$

deleting (1 + q) from this intermediate equation, we have:

$$NPV_0 = \sum_{t=0}^{N} CF_t \text{ in real prices } \cdot (1+I_{real})^{-t}.$$

In conclusion, the net present value is the same regardless of whether we use real or nominal prices, as long as the appropriate corresponding discount rate is used.

Internal Rate of Return

The internal rate of return will differ depending on whether the cash flow is stated in real or nominal prices. The equation which gives the internal rate of return for cash flow in nominal prices is:

$$0 = \sum_{t=0}^{N} CF_t \text{ in nominal prices } \cdot (1+\text{IRR}_{\text{nom}})^{-t},$$

for cash flows given in real prices it is:

$$0 = \sum_{t=0}^{N} \text{CF}_t \text{ in real prices } \cdot (1 + \text{IRR}_{\text{real}})^{-t},$$

IRR_{nom} and IRR_{real} represent the internal rate of return based on nominal prices and real prices, respectively.

We see that:

$$\text{CF}_t \text{ in nominal prices} = \text{CF}_t \text{ in real prices} \cdot (1 + q)^t$$

and from this we have:

$$\sum_{t=0}^{N} \text{CF}_t \text{ in nominal prices } \cdot (1 + q)^t \cdot (1 + \text{IRR}_{\text{nom}})^{-t} =$$

$$\sum_{t=0}^{N} \text{CF}_t \text{ in real prices } \cdot (1 + \text{IRR}_{\text{real}})^{-t}.$$

This equation is solved for:

$$(1 + \text{IRR}_{\text{nom}}) = (1 + \text{IRR}_{\text{real}}) \cdot (1 + q).$$

This means that the relationship between the internal rate of return for nominal prices and the internal rate of return for real prices is the same as the relation between the discount rates in nominal and real terms.

Year	Real price	Nominal price	Net present value in real prices (4.5 % p.a)	Net present value in nominal prices (15 % p.a.)
0				
1	10,000	11,000	9,565	9,565
2	10,000	12,100	9,149	9,149
3	10,000	13,310	8,752	8,752
4	10,000	14,641	8,371	8,371
5	10,000	16,105	8,007	8,007
			NPV_0 = 43,844	NPV_0 = 43,844
			A = 10,000	A = 13,079

Annuity

A simple relationship between the annuity in nominal prices and real prices cannot be made[1]. Consider a constant annuity in real prices of €10,000 per year, with an annual inflation of 10 % and a nominal discount rate of 15 % p.a. The discount rate in real prices would then be 4.5 % p.a. The corresponding annuity in nominal prices is dependent on the time horizon. With a time horizon of 5 years, the annuity's nominal price is €13,079, while with a time horizon of 4 years it is €12,553.

Example 6.3

After spending €5.5 million in development costs, the R&D department of IDEAS Inc. has just created a new product which is now ready for production and marketing.

An investment of €12.5 million in new production equipment is required to start production. This equipment is expected to have a lifespan of 10 years and a scrap value of zero at the conclusion of its useful life. To promote sales and encourage branding, a marketing campaign is planned for the first three years. A contract has been signed with a marketing agency which costs €2 million the first year, €1.5 million the second year, and €1 million the third year. After the three-year period the product should be well-established in the market and no further product-specific marketing will be necessary. The marketing department estimates that 100,000 units can realistically be sold in the first year at a price of €575. Annual sales volume is expected to double in each of the following years and stabilize at 500,000 units by Year 4. After the sixth year sales volume is projected to decrease by 100,000 units per year, with the tenth year being this product's final one on the market.

The direct variable production cost is €545 per unit. This covers raw materials, labor costs, and energy consumption. All other costs can be disre-

1 This is due to the fact that when cash flow is a constant annuity in real prices, the corresponding cash flow in nominal prices becomes a geometric progression with the quotient (1 + q). The amount in real prices in the tth time period must be multiplied by $(1 + q)^t$ to be converted into nominal prices.

garded. Inflation is expected to remain constant at 3 % p.a. over the next ten years and the sales prices and production costs will follow the general inflation. Also of note is that IDEAS Inc. depreciates assets at 30 % annually based on the balance method. Finally, the company applies a nominal discount rate of 12 % p.a. and pays 34 % tax.

The first step in the investment analysis is to analyze which information should be included in the investment calculation and which should be excluded. Also, a decision about whether to use real or nominal prices must be made and tax implications must be considered.

The fact that €5.5 million has been spent on product development is irrelevant, as this is a sunk cost. It does not matter what decision is made regarding future production or marketing; the money is irreversibly spent and therefore has no impact on the strategic decision about whether to bring the product to market or not.

The €12.5 million investment in production equipment is the same whether we use nominal or real prices because it is made at the start of Year 1. This investment does not factor directly in the tax calculation, but it has an impact through depreciation. Depreciation can be calculated precisely over the coming years on the basis of the investment amount and the applied depreciation scheme; depreciation will therefore be in nominal terms. There will be a capital loss write-off in Year 10 amounting to €353,094. This is equivalent to the difference between the book value at Year 10 and the expected scrap value of zero.

Year	Marketing	Units sold	Contribution-margin in real prices	Contribution-margin in nominal prices	Depreciation
1	€2,000,000	€100,000	€3,000,000	€3,090,000	€3,750,000
2	€1,500,000	€200,000	€6,000,000	€6,365,400	€2,625,000
3	€1,000,000	€400,000	€12,000,000	€13,112,724	€1,837,500
4		€500,000	€15,000,000	€16,882,632	€1,286,250
5		€500,000	€15,000,000	€17,389,111	€900,375
6		€500,000	€15,000,000	€17,910,784	€630,263
7		€400,000	€12,000,000	€14,758,486	€441,184
8		€300,000	€9,000,000	€11,400,931	€308,829
9		€200,000	€6,000,000	€7,828,639	€216,180
10		€100,000	€3,000,000	€4,031,749	€504,420

The marketing campaign has already been contractually settled with the marketing agency and will therefore be in nominal prices. Marketing costs are part of the company's operating costs and will reduce the taxable net income.

Net cash flow from sales is calculated as sales volume in units, multiplied by the sales price less direct production costs. Projected sales volumes have been set and are not influenced by inflation. However, both the sales prices and direct production costs are expected to follow the general inflationary trend of 3 % per year. So, the data for sales prices and direct production costs are given in real terms.

As mentioned, we can decide whether to develop the cash flows in nominal or real terms. In this case we will perform the investment analysis in nominal prices, meaning that net cash flow from sales (contribution margin) should be converted from real prices to nominal prices. The contribution margin in real prices is €30 per unit (€575 - €545).

On the basis of the above background data, we can calculate nominal cash flow before and after tax.

Year	Cash flow in nominal prices before tax	Tax payment	Cash flow in nominal prices after tax
0	–€12,500,000	0	–€12,500,000
1	€1,090,000	–€904,400	€185,600
2	€4,865,400	€761,736	€4,103,664
3	€12,112,724	€3,493,576	€8,619,148
4	€16,882,632	€5,302,770	€11,579,862
5	€17,389,111	€5,606,170	€11,782,941
6	€17,910,784	€5,875,377	€12,035,407
7	€14,758,486	€4,867,883	€9,890,603
8	€11,400,931	€3,771,351	€7,629,616
9	€7,828,639	€2,588,236	€5,240,403
10	€4,031,749	€1,199,292	€2,832,457

With an applied discount rate of 12 % p.a., the investment analysis yields the following result on a before-tax basis:

Net present value	= €46,054,742
Internal rate of return, IRR	= 57.7 % p.a.
Annuity	= €8,149,367 per year

If we use the cash flow after tax and apply an after-tax discount rate of 7.9 % p.a. we have:

Net present value	= €37,841,281
Internal rate of return, IRR	= 47.3 % p.a.
Annuity	= €5,619,134 per year

The investment is profitable on both a before-tax and after-tax basis.

Cash Flow and the Discount Rate

In summary, there must always be cohesiveness between the cash flow base used and the discount rate applied.

This cohesiveness is illustrated in the following schematic chart:

Cash flow	Discount rate
Nominal prices or nominal figures before tax. That is, the monetary amount in euros or some other currency which is paid at the time of transaction.	Nominal discount rate before tax: I_{nom}
Nominal prices or nominal figures after tax. In other words, the monetary amount paid at the time of transaction and adjusted for the tax payment.	Tax-adjusted nominal discount rate: $I_{nom,\ after\ tax} = I_{nom} \cdot (1 - \text{tax rate})$

Real prices or real figures before tax. Future prices exclusive of inflation. (Sometimes amounts used are expressed in terms of the current price in euros.)	Discount rate in real terms before tax: $I_{real} = \frac{1+I_{nom}}{1+q} - 1$ or $I_{real} = \frac{I_{nom} - q}{1+q}$
Real prices or real figures after tax. Future prices exclusive of inflation and adjusted for the tax payment.	Tax-adjusted discount rate in real terms: $I_{real,\ after\ tax} = \frac{I_{nom} \cdot (1-s) - q}{1+q}$

CHAPTER 7

Investment Objectives and Evaluation

Satisficing vs. maximizing

The fundamentals of classical investment theory are based on the assumption that all decision makers act rationally and possess complete knowledge and information about the various investing alternatives at hand. The consequences of their actions and future goals are fully known. This represents the so-called "economic man" approach.

This premise is the basis of the *shareholder value perspective,* which combines concepts from Corporate Finance and Corporate Strategy. It assumes that strategic decisions are made under full rationality and solely to maximize the firm's value, as measured by net present value of all the future cash flows in the form of dividends, return on invested capital and capital gains. According to the shareholder value perspective, the owners' return is maximized only when the firm carries out investments or strategies that have positive NPV, as this increases the overall market cap of the firm. This rationale is in accordance with the fundamental principle of investment theory, which states that the net present value of initiated investment projects or strategies must always be greater than zero.

This approach assumes that investments and strategies encompass relatively simple and routine decisions, and are therefore very straightforward to conduct. However, investment decisions are usually complex and cannot be characterized by routines. Decisions are often made under the pressure of time constraints and amid great uncertainty. Consequently, the strictly rationale view of investments, though it helps in developing conceptual frameworks, must be approached with caution when applied in the real world.

Aside from the complexities involved in evaluating investment strategies themselves, the needs and objectives of the various stakeholders in a company must also be considered. Yet often these needs may be different and involve conflicting expectations and goals in areas such as technology, work processes, environmental impact, market demand, risk tolerance, etc. These factors, too, can compromise the rationality of the investment decision making process.

The investment approach which seeks to reconcile these factors is called the *behavioristic perspective.* In it, organizations are regarded as a coalition of differing interests, each with its own set of expectations and requirements. These facets cannot be reduced to a single goal but rather co-exist as a set of constraints which the organization must work within. A particular investment decision, for example, must generate an acceptable return for the shareholders, yet also comply with corporate strategy directives, market demands, human resource policies, and government regulations, etc. If one proposed investment does not meet these demands sufficiently, the company will begin to search for a better alternative. Many of a firm's larger investment decisions are therefore a result of a negotiation process between its different interested stakeholders.

Even if we assume that a company's decision makers wish to make a strictly rational investment, it would be unrealistic to believe that they could gather all of the information required for a decision whose consequences and alternatives are fully known. This would be overly time consuming and expensive, if it were even possible from a creative, comprehensive search perspective. Moreover, management's capacity to process all information is not unlimited and human behavior is not always predictable and rational. And since business systems are populated by people, the systems themselves are subject to "internally generated" unpredictability. Also, intuition and judgment are in real life known to carry great weight when decisions are actually made.

In practice, the search for investing alternatives is often *sequential* and *local.* It is sequential in the sense that new alternatives are generally sought one at a time in a search that lasts only until the first acceptable option can be found. It is local because a company typically pursues new investment ideas which resemble those it has tried before. These factors introduce a cognitive bias that leads a company's executives to invest from an internally focused perspective which often excludes or overlooks those views which do not accord with their own. In general, the more limited a firm is in its creative approach to searching for alternatives, the more its alternatives will tend to be sequential and local. Another way to say this is that a company's decision makers work under uncertainty and must choose investment alternatives on this basis. This is called *satisficing* because the company at some point must reach a place where it is satisfied with a given solution, even though it realizes that a better alternative might exist. The chosen alternative is considered to be satifising, or "good enough" in relation to the required set of goals.

The consequence of relaxing the strict assumption that investment decisions are completely rational, saying instead that they are characterized by limited rationality, is that firms might accept investment decisions which yield an annual rate of return of 14 % and an NPV of €600,000 even though a more time consuming and exhaustive search could possibly have surfaced an investment whose return was 16 % per year with a net present value of €750,000.

With this in mind, we can state that investment decisions are made with the goal of maximizing shareholder value in NPV terms, given some limitations which vary from firm to firm and over time. The main objective is to ensure that these limitations are minimize and restricted to the way information is processed. In other words, it is important to be conscious of *how* the numbers in the investment calculation are determined and to ensure that the methods and assumptions used for considering investment alternatives is as complete and wide-ranging as possible. The more alternatives and scenarios a firm considers for its investment project, the more its decision making process will approach an optimum solution.

Classical investment theory assumes that future and discounted cash flows are fully known and remain constant through time. In practice, cash flows are often uncertain and rarely stable. Futhermore, the investment may be broken into phases, where the execution of each one leads to a decision on whether to complete the investment as planned, to adapt it, put it on hold, or exit it completely. It is this division of an investment into phases and possible scenario outcomes that creates an entirely new perspective. If the firm views the investment process as a series of partial decisions, each phase can be seen as an option to make an optimum decision which considers the project, information gathered and outside world. This is the best way to capture the firm's opportunities, make informed decisions and yet remain flexible in the investment process.

In this process we can also make use of classical business strategy evaluation models where elements as *suitability, feasibility and acceptability*[1] are considered. An example of a schematic outline of this model can be illustrated as below:

	Suitability		**Feasibility**			**Acceptability**			
	Issue 1	Issue 2	Finan-cial	Re-sources	Other	Finan-cial return	Risk	Stakeholder preference	
								Stake-holder A	Stake-holder B
Strategic invest-ment option A									
Strategic invest-ment option B									
Strategic invest-ment option C									

Suitability looks at whether the issues raised in the strategic analysis are actually addressed by the investment alternative. This may involve looking at issues like fit with vision, mission and objectives of the company and whether the investment strategy build on strengths and opportuni-

[1] This categorisation can also be seen as *appropriateness, feasibility and desirability* or other like definitions. The categories should be seen as a convenience only and not as cut-and-dried definitions.

ties and avoid weaknesses and threats identified in the SWOT analysis. *Feasibility* is whether the investment alternative is at all realistic to implement and whether it is capable of achieving the objectives set. The issues here are particularly focused on implementation, availability of financing and other resources, timing and if key success factors in the industry are addressed.

Finally *acceptability* looks at the acceptance and desirability of the investment strategy from the perspective of various stakeholders. The focus is here in particular the expected return and profitability compared to risk taken and an assessment of the various stakeholders' preferences in relation to the investment.

The various investment scenarios or options (here A to C) can be listed vertically and evaluated on the key elements that the decision maker lists under the headlines suitability, feasibility and acceptability.

CHAPTER 8

Real Options

The Inclusion of Strategic and Dynamic Perspectives in the Investment Calculation

One weakness of the traditional investment model is that it considers the entire investment process as static. This is true in the sense that operating decisions are assumed to be fixed in advance and that the investment's calculation consists of a base case with known, predictable cash flows. However, the world as a whole and the company itself invariably change over time, often in dramatic ways. The traditional model is therefore best suited to "now-or-never" investments with known future cash flows and passive investors who implement the proposed investment project as originally planned.

This set of circumstances rarely exists in practice, however. Instead, most companies try to be flexible in their investment decisions and implementation process. Rather than rigidly following the base-case assumptions, they tend to adapt the investment strategy over time as new information is received and the outcome of previous decisions becomes known. Examples abound. They include pharmaceutical companies engaged in research and development of new drugs; oil companies drilling for oil; automobile manufacturers planning plant capacity; and so forth. Therefore, we say that the investment decision is characterized by "real options" where the decision maker has the right, but not the obligation, to invest. This right to invest typically applies over a certain period of time and consists of a series of alternative possibilities and options. This is precisely in line with financial option theory.

Real options are therefore directly related to the uncertainty inherent in investments and to the firm's strategic response to external changes in its operating environment. This flexibility enables a firm to adapt the approach it uses when faced with uncertain market conditions. This is a key difference between the real options approach and the traditional methods. A measure of uncertainty can be introduced into inherently uncertain strategic investments.

As opposed to financial options where the focus is on financial markets, the real options approach focuses on companies and on the strategic investment decisions they make. Consequently, real options are not formally structured in the way financial options are, nor are they defined by option contracts. Instead, they consist of opportunities and actions which the firm's management must identify and implement. Real options represent a more strategic way of thinking by the firm and form a link between strategic planning and investment theory.

The word *real* is used to illustrate that the underlying asset is not a financial asset as in options theory, but a real asset in the sense of a company's property, plant, or equipment. One of the primary advantages of the real options approach is that the investment's risk can be reduced and its value increased by allowing the company to invest capital in a series of separate phases. It can invest in small increments while maintaining the flexibility to strategically adapt its approach. It does this by reconfiguring the investment plan as needed per the knowledge gleaned from each successive implementation phase. This lets the company test the investment's viability at each point, which reduces its level of risk going forward. The decision to continue investing or not in successive phases can be based on whether or not the project has attained the company's goals at that particular point in time.

By separating investments into phases a company can improve its use of the information it gathers. This creates a more logical decision process than if it were to make a comprehensive decision at the beginning of the investment project, and it increases the investment's value to shareholders. The information gathered about market demand, competition, or cost structure, for example, can lead to optimal decisions about a new product's introduction timing or the equipment capacity needed to satisfy changing production schedules. Good management is characterized by the ability to make wise investment decisions from a range of available options, promoting those with high growth potential and avoiding those which will likely lead to losses. Many managers use intuition in this way, without necessarily being able to account for it. A real option is different from intuition in that it provides a structure for this line of thought, making it visible and enhancing the decision making ability of good managers. Viewing investments as real options enables them to respond strategically and proactively to business opportunities in an uncertain environment. Real options are therefore far more of a strategic tool than a technical method because they combine financial theory with strategy in a way that adds value for the firm.

This approach is broadly applicable. For example, many product and market development projects involve decisions where a firm can choose at any point to continue its efforts, delay further investment, or completely withdraw. An ability to learn continuously as new information emerges always improves investment decisions, so the more volatile the business environment, the more useful a company will find the real options method.

Another situation where real options are helpful is when making an investment may purchase the right to future cash flows. Under the traditional investment approach, these future cash flows must be excluded since they are uncertain. This decreases the project's net present value and makes it more likely to be rejected. With real options, however, the value of these potential future cash flows can be included, which may alter the strategic decision about whether to invest or not.

The Calculation Models for Options

To quantify the real options approach we take for a conceptual starting point the two well-known models used in financial options: the Black-Scholes formula and the Binomial method.

The premise of Black-Scholes is that the investor can make decisions at different points in time, with the value of the investment subject to rise or fall a given amount according to probabilities. For example, an investor at Time 0 may consider an investment of €1 million which has a 50 % probability of increasing to €3 million at Time 1 and a 50 % chance of falling to €0.5 million in the same period. Unlike the traditional investment model, Black-Scholes uses several event spaces with different probability outcomes. The Binomial model, meanwhile, can be expanded from one time period to multiple time periods.

One of the distinctions between the two models is that the Binomial method operates in a discreet time period, while the Black-Scholes model assumes a continuous time-frame. Furthermore, the Binomial method operates with a given number of event spaces, while Black-Scholes uses a continuous event space based on outcome probabilities.

We will not go into details here about assessing options according to the Black-Scholes model, but instead focus on the practical and strategic aspects of real options. A full explanation of Black-Scholes is given in the appendix, but we note in passing that the model can very precisely and mathematically determine the value of options.

Only rarely can the outcome probabilities required by the Black-Scholes model be quantified meaningfully and precisely. For example, imagine a simplified case in which an investment project's risk is directly linked to the variance and standard deviation of the price of oil or some other raw material with a known tendency for price fluctuations. In such a case the Black-Scholes formula would be usable, but few investment projects have this type of information so precisely known.

In addition, Black-Scholes assumes that the right to the option is exclusive to the decision maker and that competitors or others cannot take advantage of the opportunity. This is not necessarily the case with real options.

For these reasons, the Black-Scholes model is not feasible for most real-life investment projects. However, we can use it as a starting point to understand the mindset behind real options and then combine this understanding with the decision tree approach which we will introduce shortly.

Real Options in Practice

As mentioned, it is very important that an investing company assess the staging of its investment decisions and the background circumstances which will come into play. In assessing real options a practical approach should be used consisting of the following steps:

1. Calculate the base case's net present value without options.
2. Perform a risk assessment using scenario analysis.
3. Identify management's options (i.e. project flexibility).
4. Create a decision tree reflecting the scenarios.
5. Calculate the project's expected NPV using the decision tree (Excel).

We will now look into the way that giving a decision maker the chance to avoid proceeding with an investment actually offers value to the project:

Example 8.1
Gamma Inc. is on the verge of a new project, which requires €1 million in start-up costs and an additional €5 million one year from now (t=1) to complete it. In the best-case scenario, the project has a 60 % probability of generating a first-year net present value of €9 million in future cash flows.

Meanwhile, there is a 40 % chance that the worst-case scenario of €1 million in NPV of future cash flows at this time (t=1) will be realized.

In the traditional weighted-average investment model, the investment project is considered static. We factor in the probabilities for both scenarios using a discount factor of 10 % per year and predict a total net present value for the investment project of:

$$NPV_0 = -1{,}000{,}000 - 5{,}000{,}000 \cdot 1.1^{-1} + 9{,}000{,}000 \cdot 1.1^{-1} \cdot 60\,\% + 1{,}000{,}000 \cdot 1.1^{-1} \cdot 40\,\% = € -272{,}727.$$

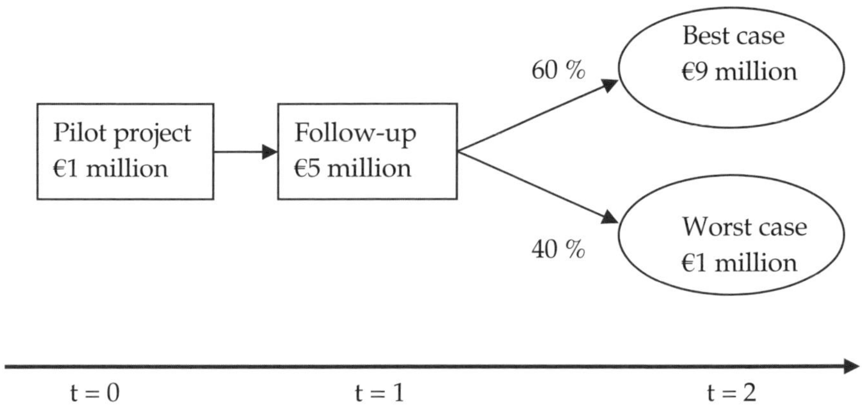

Figure 8.1 Investment decision tree

Let us now factor in the value of the flexibility by dividing the project into two phases. First we invest €1 million in the pilot project at t=0. Then we wait until t=1 to decide whether or not to invest the remaining €5 million needed to complete the project. If we factor in the option to cancel the project at t=1, the calculation would look like this:

$$NPV_0 = -1{,}000{,}000 + (9{,}000{,}000 - 5{,}000{,}000) \cdot 1.1^{-1} \cdot 60\ \%$$
$$+ 0 \cdot 1.1^{-1} \cdot 40\ \% = €\ 1{,}181{,}818.$$

The opportunity to cancel the investment project at t=1 clearly has a value. The investment in the pilot project at t=0 not only gives the option to reap the benefits of a good investment, but also the opportunity to reduce a potential loss by not investing further at t=1 if the project turns out poorly. Therefore, using the real options approach, the NPV calculation reveals a hidden value in the project which stems from the company's ability to be flexible.

As mentioned earlier, for investments with higher risk there is a value in being able to delay investments until better information exists. This lets the information be adapted in an optimal way. We will now look at an isolated investment of €5 million to complete the project.

Example 8.2

Gamma Inc. can invest €5 million to complete the development of its project. As in Example 7.1, the project has a 60 % probability of generating a best-case NPV value of €9 million in future cash flows at t=1 and a 40 % probability of generating a worst-case return of only € 1 million in the same time period.

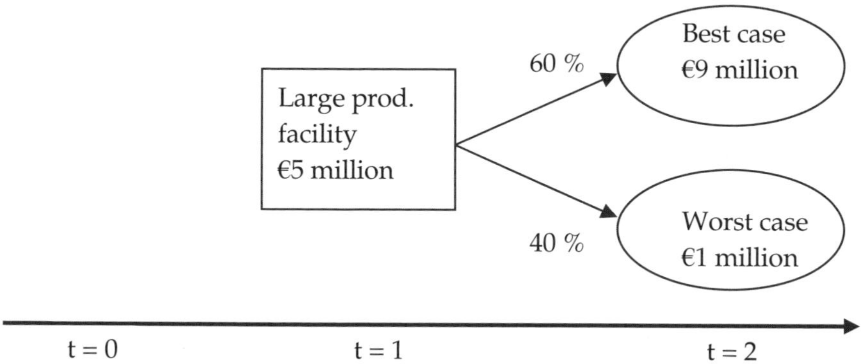

Figure 8.2 the investment's decision tree

The traditional model would yield an expected value at t=1 of:

$$NPV_{0,t=1} = -5{,}000{,}000 + 9{,}000{,}000 \cdot 60\ \% + 1{,}000{,}000 \cdot 40\ \% = €800{,}000.$$

Looked at in isolation, the completion of the investment project is viable at t=1, but also risky. This is reflected in its relatively low return of €800,000. However, if we factor in Gamma Inc.'s ability to delay the project from t=1 to t=2 and assume that the best-case probability increases to 80 % because of strategic changes in the intervening year, the expected net present value at t=2 becomes:

$$NPV_{0,t=1} = -5{,}000{,}000 \cdot 1.1^{-1} + 9{,}000{,}000 \cdot 1.1^{-1} \cdot 80\ \% + 1{,}000{,}000 \cdot 1.1^{-1} \cdot 20\ \% = €1{,}818{,}182.$$

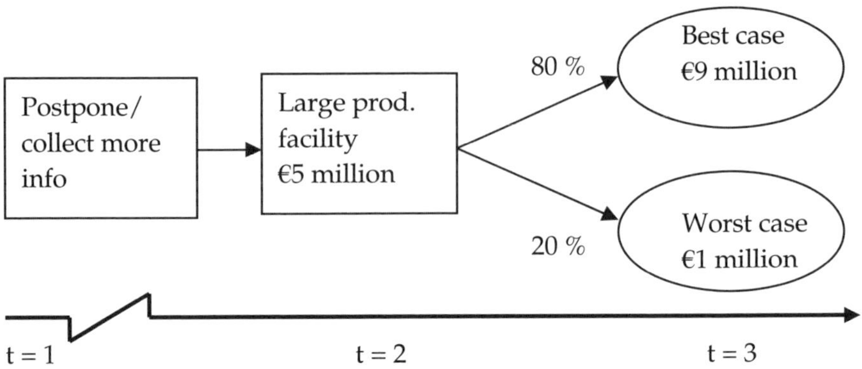

Figure 8.3 the investment's decision tree with a delay

In other words, if Gamma is not convinced at t=1 that the project's expected return of €800,000 is enough to cover its risk, there is a potential value in delaying the €5 million investment until t=2 and using the extra year to gather more information. This will let Gamma try to time the investment better and avoid the worst-case scenario outcome. The value of Gamma's delaying the follow-up investment needs to be weighed against the cost of gathering additional information and the risk that competitors might preempt it in the market. Both possibilities would decrease the company's return on the investment.

This example illustrates that the option to react to information strategically adds value to the investment process. By investing smaller amounts of money in the initial phases of the investment, the firm gains valuable flexibility in the form of real options since it can then either continue investing later or cancel, adjust or delay the project.

The decision about whether a company proceeds with further investment in a project can be based on the way resources like fixed assets, managerial talent, production experience, R&D capability and market power are deployed in the initial investment.

This knowledge about using real options in investment decisions can now be expanded to a practical model which considers the case where a company reacts strategically to opportunities that arise from new information and changes in the external environment.

Example 8.3

Our firm Gamma Inc. is considering development of an entirely new product. The costs associated with the necessary permits and project start-up is estimated at €1 million and will last an entire year. At year's end the company will have to decide, based on information it has gathered from market testing and an updated assessment of its operating environment, whether or not to bring the product to market. We assume that Gamma has the following options after the first year:

1. Invest an additional €5 million to establish a large production facility.
2. Invest €3 million to establish a smaller production facility.
3. Cancel or delay the project due to negative investment prospects.

For the sake of clarity, we will assume that if Gamma invests additional funds at either capacity level, both a best-case and a worst-case will be possible at the end of t=1. The probabilities will be the same in both instances: 80 % for the best-case and 20 % for the worst-case. This implies four outcome possibilities.

For each outcome possibility a net present value can be calculated based on the respective future cash flows at t=1. These calculations are relatively simple because Gamma can alter the decision's critical input variables such as sales volume and fixed costs, then adjust the cash flows accordingly.

Essentially, this is equivalent to an expanded scenario analysis which includes the opportunity to make strategic decisions (in this case, construct a large or small production facility).

The total net present value in t = 0 is:

$$
\begin{aligned}
NPV_{0/t=0} = & -1{,}000{,}000 \\
& + 60\,\% \cdot (-5{,}000{,}000 + 9{,}000{,}000 \cdot 80\,\% + 1{,}000{,}000 \cdot 20\,\%) \cdot 1.1^{-1} \\
& + 30\,\% \cdot (-3{,}000{,}000 + 5{,}000{,}000 \cdot 80\,\% + 1{,}000{,}000 \cdot 20\,\%) \cdot 1.1^{-1} \\
& + 10\,\% \cdot 0 \qquad\qquad = €\,636{,}364.
\end{aligned}
$$

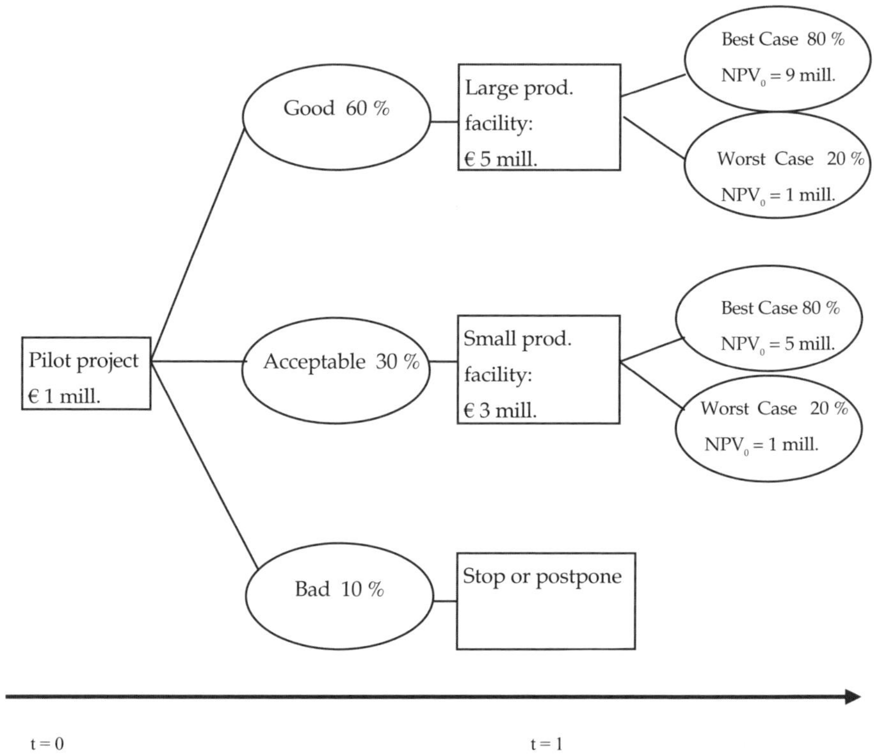

Figure 8.4 Decision tree with options for investment alternatives

This analysis can obviously be expanded. For example, if Gamma decides to construct a small production facility at t=1 but later sees that a larger plant is desirable, it can expand capacity further in t=2. The investment decision tree and would then be created as follows:

If Gamma constructs a smaller production facility at t=1, a decision to expand or not will be made at t=2. This will depend on how the market has developed. The NPV calculation will consider this impact and the scenario which dominates will be the one with the greater economic value.

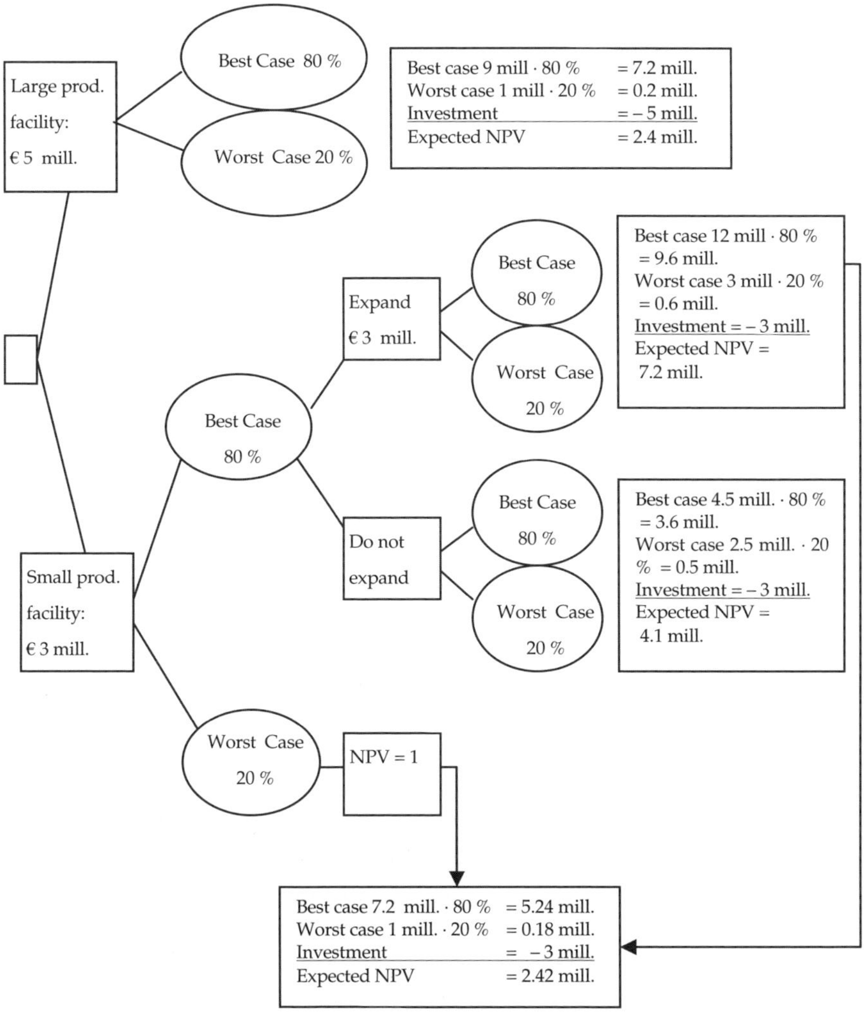

Figure 8.5 Investment decision tree with options between alternatives

To make this determination we analyze what the decision maker will do at t=2, given that a smaller facility has already been built. If the market is favorable and we invest the €3 million required for expansion, Gamma will realize a €12 million gain one year later with an 80 % probability, or a €3 million profit with 20 % probability. The total expected net present value for this decision at t=2 is therefore:

$$NPV_{0,t=2} = -3{,}000{,}000 + 12{,}000{,}000 \cdot 80\,\% + 3{,}000{,}000 \cdot 20\,\% = €7{,}200{,}000.$$

If Gamma does not expand, the net present value at t=2 is:

$$NPV_{0,t=2} = 4{,}500{,}000 \cdot 80\,\% + 2{,}500{,}000 \cdot 20\,\% = €\,4{,}100{,}000.$$

Consequently, if the market develops favorably after t=1, the expected net present value of expanding production dominates the value of not expanding. The rational investor will choose the dominant strategy and opt to increase capacity. The expected NPV at t=2 is therefore €7,200,000.

Knowing this, we work backwards to analyze the decision existing at t=1.

The net present value of constructing a small facility is calculated as:

$$NPV_{0,t=1} = -3{,}000{,}000 + 7{,}200{,}000 \cdot 80\,\% \cdot 1.1^{-1} + 1{,}000{,}000 \cdot 20\,\% \cdot 1.1^{-1}$$
$$= €2{,}420{,}000.$$

If Gamma chooses to build a large facility the NPV is:

$$NPV_{0,t=1} = -5{,}500{,}000 + 9{,}000{,}000 \cdot 80\,\% + 1{,}000{,}000 \cdot 20\,\% = €2{,}400{,}000.$$

In this particular case it is marginally the best strategy - with €20,000 - to go for the smaller facility, watch how the market develops in each year, and react strategically at each point in the most rational way possible.

In other words, if the €1 million pilot phase investment has a "good", Gamma should invest in the large production facility at t=1. If the result is "acceptable", it should opt for the smaller facility. If it does, we have already incorporated the possibility of expanding production later on should the market develop favorably after Year 1 (see the previous calculation of the dominant strategy).

The analogy in this example can be extended to include the following:

- Firms which gain access to a new market through an initial investment.
  Examples include mergers and acquisitions or geographic expansions.
- Agricultural companies which introduce a test crop into a new area or try to increase their existing farmland's harvest.
- IT firms which launch a new application but wait for the market's reaction before investing in the development of software upgrades.
- Organizations which perform feasibility studies to gain insights into how their investment might perform so that they can make a well-considered decision at t=1.
- Real estate investments where the property's use can be adapted to match the demands of the market.
- Pharmaceutical companies which conduct costly research and development and must then make production launch decisions in accordance with a rational strategy.

One limitation of the traditional investment model is that it often underestimates the value of projects with strategic implications for the company. This is because the ability to make follow-on investments in projects with high growth potential cannot be factored in. With real options, however, this growth and its value to the company can be evaluated.

In using real options, then, the company must understand what result the strategic actions under its control will have if the investment is made.

Deciding which of these actions are feasible and will have a significant beneficial impact is therefore an important part of using real options. Examples may include the following:

- Price response to competitor actions.
- Product changes.
- Speed of capacity expansions.
- Market timing.

Let us consider Gamma again, whose products are already leading the market in Europe, North America, and South America. It is considering expanding into Asia by acquiring a company in Thailand engaged in similar activities. The geographical expansion will not be easy for Gamma because the Thai market is fiercely competitive. Smaller companies will respond aggressively to any new threats they see.

Using the traditional method, the Thai expansion has a negative net present value based on its future cash flows. Yet considering the project in isolation does not consider the future growth which Gamma may realize by making this initial investment. By gaining access to market in Thailand and successfully differentiating its products, Gamma may be able to expand into other parts of Asia, and real options can evaluate the impact of this potential.

Therefore we ought to determine the value of an investment decision or strategy as:

> Value of traditional statistic investment calculation + value of real option.

In other words, the traditional investment method must be supplemented by the value of the option whenever the company is faced with a high-risk project or is able to stage the investment over time in response to internal and external strategic factors. We do not dismiss the traditional investment method. Rather, we supplement it with real option because a company's ability to alter its strategy in response to new information can greatly enhance the investment's value.

Final Considerations

As we conclude the discussion of real options, some key points to remember are as follows:

1. The value of having real options depends on how well a company can gather strategic information about a project over time.
2. If an investment can be delayed, the ability to wait has value. The longer the delay that is possible the greater the impact be-

cause the company can see if a more favorable investment scenario develop. This assumes that the investment opportunity remains the same over time.

3. Real options are more valuable for projects of higher risk. If an investment has strong growth potential but significant risk of loss, real options allow the project to be funded in stages. Follow-up investments are made only if those made previously do well; otherwise the project can be discontinued or further investment postponed, all for much less money than if a full investment had been made up-front. One caveat is that a riskier investment carries a higher discount rate for valuation purposes, which decreases the present value of future cash flows. This means that the real options (which spread cash flows over time) would have a lower net present value than those resulting from the traditional investment method. In this case the true benefit of the options cannot be weighed since the increased value of the real option may or may not compensate for the reduction in net present value.
4. The value of real options depends on whether a firm has an exclusive right to the options, or whether others can use them. If the options are available to competitors, their value is naturally lower. In this case a company's tendency would be to begin the investment early. This aspect of an option's exclusivity plays an especially important role when the project's net present value is large or when competition is strong and other companies can easily use the option.

CHAPTER 9

International Investments

Perspectives and Considerations in International Investment Strategies

In recent years, economies around the world have become increasingly interconnected. One result of this globalization is that investment projects frequently assume an international dimension. Typical business drivers of this focus are as follows:

- Access to growth markets.
- Access to resources (oil, raw materials, human resources, etc.).
- Opportunities for efficiency improvement (lower cost structures, efficiency gains, economies of scale).
- Supply chain proximity to key suppliers or customers. For example a company may start a venture in Asia because its primary customer is Japanese and wants its supplier base nearby.

Other real-life drivers of international investment strategies may be strong domestic competition from overseas firms, management ambition, and unsolicited proposals which management finds attractive.

As in any investment decision, scenario building and strategic planning are helpful tools in evaluating an international opportunity. Actually creating those options can be complicated and requires careful, creative deal structures. However, in general terms it is simple: The company should invest in a way that gives it the right, but not the obligation, to make additional investments at some point in the future. The primary investment structures include the following types:

- Acquisition (full or partial).
- Joint venture.
- Greenfield (independent start-up venture).

If an acquisition strategy is used, it often provides quick access to strategically important local resources. However, it can also lead to significant unexpected expenses once two different organizations and business styles try to meld. Organizational tension, communication styles, and the departure of key managers may diminish the operational gains which investors had expected. This risk is especially great when the two companies have substantial cultural differences. Empirical research shows that firms undertaking international acquisitions usually underestimate the post-merger integration costs. The greater the culture differences, the greater the cost overruns tend to be.

Acquisition through partial ownership is a means of creating real options on strategic business elements. Follow-on investments which are contingent upon the initial stage's success may be made. This approach allows a company to both conserve capital and remain in control of its investment. Unlike joint ventures, which typically involve two investing parties, purchasing a partial equity stake in a more widely held company can create the required degree of control through a much lower level of investment.

In a joint venture the investing parties combine the complementary pieces of their companies into a new entity without one party having to acquire the other. This provides an entering firm with access to the local partners' resources, which may include local knowledge, vendor and customer networks, market access, and technology. Because both companies remain independent, there is less risks of post-merger integration difficulties. Investment costs, meanwhile, are shared with the joint venture partner, which reduces financial risk. On the negative side, there is shared ownership, with a correspondingly lower degree of control. This often leads to disagreements between the two parties over management issues, proprietary knowledge build-up, and the handling of cultural conflicts. The relationship between joint venture partners can be highly competitive and potentially dysfunctional, which contributes to their notorious instability.

The greenfield approach is usually characterized by a more gradual market entry. As local demand develops, the firm increases its level of investment.

When considering international investments from the real options perspective, joint ventures are the most interesting of those described above.

Real options make it possible to gather valuable information about the new market and the local partner's core competency and opportunistic behavior, all with lowered risk. The larger the uncertainty about these factors the more useful the real options approach becomes.

Joint ventures can be seen as risky because proprietary knowledge must be shared as the two parties cooperate. As the local partner gains insight into this information, the exclusive right to it diminishes, which diminishes its value. On the other hand, the entering company also benefits as it acquires local knowledge and market access. A joint venture can therefore be seen as a strong way to explore strategic real options from all joint venture parties' perspective. If handled right, this can reduce the investment's overall cost and risk.

International investments in developed countries are usually done by acquisition. Those in emerging markets, meanwhile, tend to be joint ventures or greenfield start-ups. There are several reasons for this. The first is that lesser developed countries, by their very nature, have fewer suitable acquisition targets. Therefore an entering company must be prepared to start a new project alone or find a viable joint venture partner to share the investment risk. The second is that shared risk is more desirable if the outcome is more uncertain, which is often the case in emerging markets. Thirdly, the financial markets in poorer countries are often are less efficient and less developed, which makes acquisitions more difficult to structure. Finally, some nations – China, for example – have laws which prevent foreigners from owning companies outright. Instead they require a local partner, which implies a joint venture structure.

Research on the way companies choose to arrange their international investments confirms that decisions are not always made on the rational basis which investment theory assumes. Companies often execute an opportunity and simultaneously create a structure to manage it. Furthermore, their decisions are usually of the "emerging strategy" type, which means they continuously adapt their approach as new information is gathered.

International investments add a number of additional considerations in regard to cash flow estimation and risk evaluation. In regards to cash flow estimation some of these are as follows:

- Exchange rate fluctuations.
- Exchange controls.
- Differing tax rates and tax laws.

As for risk evaluation, international investments have risks that are inherently different from domestic opportunities. These arise from the different governments, laws, cultures, business norms, etc. which exist between the home country and foreign nation. The greater the differences the greater the risks will be. Some are given below:

- Political / country risk.
- Legal structure / respect for the rule of law.
- Resource base structure (human capital, distribution efficiency, etc.).
- Cultural and language barrier.

Many of these risks can be mitigated. The political risk of expropriation, for instance, which many oil companies are facing in Venezuela, can be insured against through specialized export credit institutions. This may lower the investment risk considerably, but it comes with a cost – that of the insurance premium.

As globalization increase and with it the pressure for firms to be more innovative and flexible, a one-sided focus on the traditional investment model is counterproductive because it underestimates the value of the company's potential international business opportunities. The reason is that the traditional discounting model assigns a higher interest rate to projects with higher risks, which diminishes the value of future cash flows. This creates a paradox. Greater risk increases the value of a company's real options because the potential for upside is greater, but the financial valuation is lower. Another factor which is excluded is the value a company gains when its international investment lays the foundation for future growth or further product expansion. Even if it the initial phase investment is small, this represents a real option which needs to be included in the project's financial valuation.

CHAPTER 10

Financing

Types of Finance

Companies and organizations require financing in order to carry out their strategies and investments schemes. It is important they ensure that liquidity remains positive at all times. Financing can be raised and structured in many ways, and ingenuity and creativity are needed to create the optimal financing arrangement. Raising and structuring capital involves the following aspects: Determining the best capital structure, identifying and contracting the most suitable type of financing, and ensuring the lowest possible cost of capital given a set of limiting constraints.

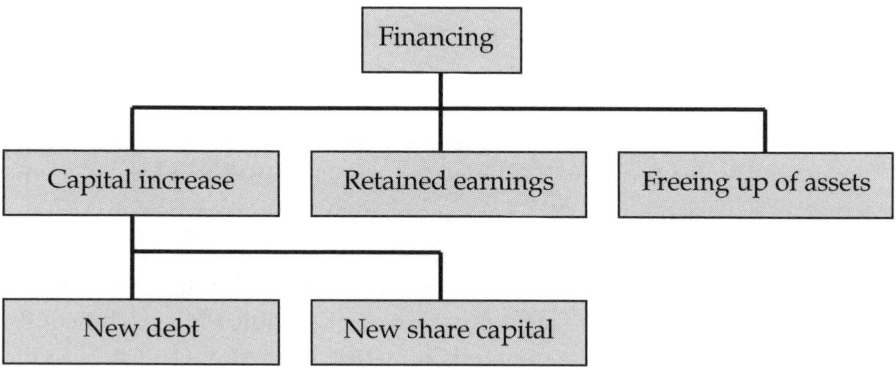

A company's financing can be sourced both externally and internally. External financing means that the money supplied is from sources outside the company, such as new or existing shareholders or banks and financial institutions. Internal financing means that the company itself generates the required funds, either through accumulation of retained earnings, divestiture of assets, or otherwise freeing up existing capital held in current or fixed assets. This can be illustrated below:

Financing decisions and structures are reflected on the liabilities side of a company's balance sheet. Simply put, the liabilities side is composed of equity and debt. Debt can then be separated into short-term and long-term debt. Meanwhile, the asset side of the balance sheet shows how a company's financing has been invested in fixed assets and current assets. This can be depicted in a simple overview as follows:

Balance sheet	
Assets	Liabilities
Fixed assets Current assets	Equity Debt - Short-term - Long-term

When deciding upon the type of financing to employ, a company should consider the balance sheet's vertical and horizontal balance structure. The vertical balance structure deals with the ratio between debt and equity, or the so-called financial gearing. The higher the ratio between debt and equity, the more highly geared or leveraged the company will be. Financially speaking, it makes sense to increase financial gearing as long as the effective marginal cost of debt is lower than the return which can be made with the incremental money. However, increased financial gearing increases the company's financial risk and therefore comes at a price, in the sense that the company becomes more vulnerable to adverse business changes. At the same time, the marginal cost of capital will gradually increase as the company raises additional amounts of capital through borrowing, because lenders face a greater risk of default as the debt/equity ratio rises and therefore demand a higher interest rate. The specific debt/equity ratio that a company prefers reflects the risk preference of its managers and stockholders, as well as the nature of its business. Therefore, management must make a deliberate choice as to its preferred vertical balance structure, taking into consideration all strategic elements and stakeholders.

The balance sheet's horizontal balance structure is concerned with comparing the cash flow stream of the financing to the cash flow stream of the assets. The focus here is on liquidity and on ensuring that the sources and uses of funds are matched in the best possible way, both in regard to timing and amounts. This means, for instance, that assets which stretch the cash flow stream far into the future should be matched with long-term debt financing, so that liquidity is preserved.

Based on these considerations, we divide financing into two main categories:

- Equity.
- Debt.

A key financial decision to be made concerns the question, how much of the total financing should be structured as equity and how much should be structured as debt? The answer requires an understanding of how the various financing possibilities impact liquidity. This decision directly impacts the company's cost of capital, and therefore the discount rate to be applied.

Companies generally raise capital in three primary ways: From undistributed profits, borrowing funds, and the sale of stock. Their marginal cost of capital is a weighted average of the cost to raise these various types of funds. This leads to a fundamental concept in finance known as the weighted average cost of capital, or WACC. It is defined as the weighted average cost of debt capital and equity capital and is given by the following equation:

$$WACC = w_d k_d + w_e k_e.$$

The variables w_d and w_e are the proportions of debt and equity in the company's capital structure and k_d and k_e represent the respective costs of debt and equity. These two types of financing are discussed separately below.

Equity

A company's equity is composed primarily of accumulated retained earnings and paid-in share capital. These represent internal and external sources of financing, respectively, and an explanation of each is given below:

1. Accumulated retained earnings: These are generated when a company's dividend payment to shareholders is less than the profit it generates. It assumes that the company has a profit and that it uses at least a part of it to finance new activities. This is known as internal or self-financing.
2. Paid-in share capital: This represents funds raised through additional capital contributions from new or existing shareholders. It increases the number of shares in a company and is known as external financing.

Stock price

The stock price of a company is the value its stock trades for on a stock exchange at any given point in time. The face value of a stock is the nominal value originally attached to one share. It is not directly related to the stock price and can vary from company to company. For example, we may have a stock which trades for €10 but has a face value of €1; another stock may trade for €10,000 but have a face value of €1,000. Both shares have the same stock price per euro of share capital, namely €10 for every €1 in nominal value. The company's total value of shares is then calculated by multiplying the number of outstanding shares by the current share price. This is known as the market capitalization.

A company's stock price is a reflection of the value placed on the stock by the stock market. In that sense we cannot talk about a "real" or "true" value, nor can we directly link the share price with the asset value of the company. Rather, the price reflects the market's expectations for the company's future cash flow. This means that a stock's share price can be over-valued or under-valued, depending on the market's expectations and assumptions. For example, think back to the stock prices of internet stocks immediately before the "dot-com bubble" burst in 2000. They were dramatically over-valued and subsequently crashed. Valuation of shares is a complex issue covered comprehensively in specialized finance books, so we will not expand on it in this book.

A company can increase its amount of equity by several different means, each of which leads to different cash flow consequences. For instance, there are three principal ways in which a company can expand its equity by issuing shares:

1. Bonus shares.
2. New stock with privileged subscription rights for existing shareholders.
3. New stock without privileged subscription rights (i.e., common stock).

These three ways of expanding equity will be discussed briefly in the following sections.

Bonus shares

Issuing *bonus shares* does not inject new capital into a company. Also called a stock split, it instead represents a capital transfer within the company's existing equity structure because it moves capital out of retained earnings and into the share capital account. Therefore it does not affect shareholder value as such. For example, assume that a company has retained earnings of €250 million and a total share capital of €500 million (5 million shares at €100 face value). Issuing bonus shares for €100 million will have the following effect:

	Before	**After**
Share capital	€500 mill.	€600 mill.
Retained earnings	€250 mill.	€150 mill.
Total equity	€750 mill.	€750 mill.
Number of shares	5 mill.	6 mill.
Price per share	€150	€125

After the transaction, the company's total equity remains the same, as does the individual shareholders' portion of the company's equity. Therefore, the issuing of bonus shares has a different purpose from raising capital, having more to do with behavioral psychology than finance.

Shareholders react positively to receiving shares for "free", even though the total value of their stock holding has not changed. Even so, there can be a number of positive factors connected with an issue of bonus shares. For example, the company will often maintain the same payout ratio, which means that the individual shareholder will receive a larger dividend because he holds more shares. Suppose that the company in the example above previously paid an annual dividend of 10 %. If it maintains this payout policy, it will pay €60 million in dividends, as opposed to the previous €50 million per year. For the individual shareholder, this increases the dividends by 20 %. Also, after the additional shares are issued the stock price will fall from 150 to 125, which will make the shares easier to sell and buy. Finally, experience shows that the market tends to react positively to issuance of bonus shares, and the share price therefore falls less than what would be expected from a purely technical calculation. Naturally, this increases the market value of the shares held by investors, which provides additional value to the individual shareholders.

Share capital increase with privileged subscription rights

When a company executes a share capital increase with privileged subscription rights, it means that the current shareholders have a right to purchase shares at the offered subscription price. Suppose that the company above needs to source an additional €100 million. It plans to do this by issuing new shares with privileged subscription rights for existing shareholders in a proportion 5 to 1. This means that for every 5 shares owned, an investor has the right to purchase one new share. If we assume that the offer price is €105 per €100 of nominal share value (€5 used for transaction costs), the change to the equity structure will be as follows:

	Before	After
Share capital	€500 mill.	€600 mill.
Reserves	€250 mill.	€250 mill.
Total Equity	€750 mill.	€850 mill.
Number of shares	5 mill.	6 mill.
Price per share	€150	€141.67

From the investor's point of view (assuming he has 5 shares) the situation will be as follows:

	Before	After
Number of shares	5	6
Price per share	€150	€141.67
Value of shares	€750	€850

The total value of the shares held by the investor grows from €750 to €850, which corresponds exactly to the increased payment he made if the company's issuing costs are ignored.

If the shareholder chooses not to exercise his subscription right, this right can be sold normally. In this example, the price of the subscription right is €41.67, since €141.67 - €100.00 nominal share value = €41.67. This means that the buyer of the subscription right will be able to buy a share for €141.67, which corresponds exactly to the new market price of the share. Again, transaction costs related to the share issuance are ignored. For the existing shareholder, this will cause the following change:

	Before	After
Number of shares	5	5
Price per share	€150	€141.67
Sale of subscription right		€41.67
Value	€750	€750

Existing shareholders are thus indemnified from the fall in share price through the opportunity to sell their privileged subscription right.

Share capital increase with free subscription

A company can raise additional capital by floating *new shares on the free market*. This means of equity financing is especially used in connection with Initial Public Offerings (IPOs). In situations where there is no direct historical financial data available, the valuation of shares from an IPO will depend strongly upon investors' expectations about the company's ability to create profits and cash flow in the future. Share prices may therefore deviate significantly from the issue price shortly after the stock has begun trading on the market.

A company's decision to raise additional financing by expanding equity is a complicated subject that involves a number of considerations, one of which pertains to the financial gearing. If the company's return on invested capital exceeds its cost of debt, there is a surplus return (spread) for the equity holders. On the other hand, if its return on capital is less than the price of debt, equity holders will be forced to accept a smaller return because the burden of debt is high.

Assume a company has €2 million in capital, split evenly between equity and debt.

It is paying 8 % annual interest on its debt and after-tax profit is €200,000, corresponding to a return on total capital of 10 % per year. Thus, out of this €200,000 sum, €80,000 was used to pay interest on the debt. This means that the remaining €120,000 represents a return on equity of 12 %. If the company had the opportunity to increase debt by an additional €1 million and still have the same 10 % return on total capital, its profit would rise to €300,000. Of this, €160,000 would have to be paid as interest on debt, leaving €140,000 for shareholders and a return on equity of 14 % p.a. This demonstrates how the company would benefit from financial gearing.

Naturally, the opposite situation would occur if the return on total capital were less than 8 % p.a. In this case, return on debt would still be 8 % p.a., so the return on equity would have to be less than 8 % p.a.

Another important consideration with regard to financial gearing is the fact that a high debt/equity ratio makes a company more sensitive to changes in market conditions. In an adverse business climate this can be critical, because the obligation to service the debt is undiminished. As revenues decrease, high debt payments can place the company under severe cash flow constraints. If a company has a low financial gearing, however, it does not have the same degree of strain. It can respond to the changed environment simply by choosing not to pay dividends, or to reduce them, since carry no burden of obligation.

Debt

Debt financing can take many forms and should be carefully evaluated with regard to cost, liquidity, risk, and flexibility. The cost evaluation of various debt opportunities is little different from the methods used to analyze investment alternatives. The task is essentially the same – the cash flows occurring at different points in time must be compared. The main distinction between investment analysis and debt financing relates to the sequence of cash inflows and outflows. Whereas an *investment* typically begins with a cash outflow followed by cash inflows, *debt financing* is the other way around; it begins with a cash inflow followed by a cash outflow. Therefore, we can use the same methods to evaluate financing opportunities which we have used previously to evaluate investment possibilities:

1. Net Present Value.
2. Internal Rate of Return, (or, in financing, effective cost of debt).
3. Annuity.

Though the methods are the same, the decision criteria will change since we are evaluating the cost of financing instead of an investment's profitability. With investments, we know that the NPV should be positive and as large as possible. In principle, we desire the same thing for financing. However, as it is very rare for financing to have a positive present value, so our task is therefore to identify the financing whose net present value is the least negative. Likewise, whereas the internal rate of return for an investment should be as high as possible, it should be as low as possible for financing. Finally, because the net present value of financing is normally negative, the annuity will also be negative. Therefore we want to find the financing opportunity with the least negative annuity.

Debt financing involves the repayment of principal according to an agreed-upon repayment schedule. Interest is payable at the end of each specified interest period – normally monthly, quarterly, or semi-annually. It is based on a fixed percentage rate or a variable (floating) rate which is determined at the start of each interest period. This rate is applied to the principal, or outstanding loan balance, at the start of the interest period.

The Effective Cost of Debt or Effective Rate of Interest

When comparing alternative financing solutions, the cost of capital is a key parameter to consider. We usually talk about the effective cost of debt, or yield, which is the effective interest rate that must be paid to hold the debt. The concept is similar to an investment's internal rate of return. Therefore the effective cost of debt is the value of R that exactly satisfies the following equation:

$$\boldsymbol{NetProceeds_0 = \sum_{t=1}^{N} Instalment_t \cdot (1+R)^{-t}} \;,$$

NP_0 is the net proceeds which the borrower receives once all the costs and fees of raising the loan have been paid. $Installment_t$ is the future payment required to repay the loan over N years and includes the repayment of both principal and interest.

The equation indicates that *the effective interest rate of debt is the exact interest rate which creates equilibrium between the loan's net proceeds and the discounted value of future installment payments.* These calculations can often be done with precision because loan documents generally stipulate the installment schedule and conditions clearly.

The loan's net proceeds are equal to the loan principal minus any capital loss, establishment costs, fees, commissions, duties, etc. The net proceeds therefore refers to the amount which the borrower actually receives as a cash disbursement on the loan. Future payments consist of loan repayments and interest plus any fees, administrative costs, contributions, etc.

Different Sub-types of Debt Finance

In the following section, we will describe the key characteristics of several types of financing types which are commonly used. It is important to note, however, that the lender and corporate borrower are free to agree upon whatever type of repayment schedule they would like. This agreement does not necessarily have to correspond to any of the main types mentioned below; in fact, it is very common to tailor a financing plan to the individual borrower's specific needs.

Non-amortizing loan or bond (bullet loan)

Bullet loans are a type of financing where there are no installment payments made during the life of the loan. Instead, the entire principal is repaid at the expiration or maturity of the loan. Interest is either paid regularly during the life of the loan, or added to the principal and paid at expiration. In the case where interest is paid regularly, we can modify the equilibrium equation above so that:

$$NP_0 = \sum_{t=1}^{N} Instalment_t \cdot (1+R)^{-t} .$$

becomes:

$$NP_0 = P \cdot R_{nom} \cdot PVIFA_{R,N} + P \cdot (1 + R)^{-N}.$$

where

NP_0	is the net proceeds.
P	is the principal.
R_{nom}	is the nominal interest rate p.a.
R	is the effective interest rate p.a.
N	is the number of years.

$P \cdot R_{nom}$ is the amount of interest to be paid per year. At a fixed nominal rate of interest, this amount is constant over the entire period of the loan. It can therefore be discounted, like an annuity would be. The principal of the loan is added to this and discounted back N years.

The financing could also be provided in a bond structure. A bond is a debt instrument with a stated "par" value, also known as nominal or face value. The bond entitles the holder to receive a fixed "coupon", or percentage of the face value, which is paid during each "coupon period" until maturity. For its part, the coupon period may be annual, semi-annual, or the like.

If the loan is structured as a bond, we can calculate the bond price:

$$\text{Bond price} = \frac{NP_0}{P} = R_{nom} \cdot PVIFA_{R,N} + (1 + R)^{-N}.$$

Therefore the bond price equals the net proceeds for every €1 of principal.

If interest is added to the principal during a bond's lifetime, the total repayment at expiration must be calculated by adding accumulated interest to the principal. This is done by compounding the principal for N years at the nominal interest rate, then discounting it back to Time 0 at the effective interest rate so that it balances against the net proceeds:

$$NP_0 = P \cdot (1 + R_{nom})^N \cdot (1 + R)^{-N}.$$

or

$$\text{Bond price} = (1 + R_{nom})^N \cdot (1 + R)^{-N} = \left(\frac{1+R_{nom}}{1+R}\right)^N.$$

This can be written as:

$$\text{Bond price} = \frac{R_P}{R} + \frac{R - R_P}{R \cdot (1+R)^N}.$$

Example 10.1
Mr. Brown wants to buy a house. He would like to finance a portion of it and has been offered a €300,000 mortgage bond with bullet repayment.

Bond price	98
Interest rate	Nominal 6 % p.a., accrued at 1.5 % quarterly
Lifetime	30 years with interest payments every quarter
Fees	€3,650
Duty stamp	1.5 % of principal
Administration fee	€200 per quarter for the lifetime of the loan

We would like to calculate the effective interest rate or yield to maturity on this financing. We do this by equating net proceeds with the discounted value of all future payments:

$$NP_0 = (P \cdot R_{nom} + \text{admin.}) \cdot PVIFA_{R,N} + P \cdot (1 + R)^{-N}.$$

$$285{,}850 = (300{,}000 \cdot 0.015 + 200) \cdot PVIFA_{120,N} + 300{,}000 \cdot (1 + R)^{-120}.$$

The yield to maturity is 1.6575 % per quarter, or an effective rate of 6.8 % p.a. This calculation is performed by a financial calculator or by using the solver function in Microsoft Excel.

If interest is compounded and added to the principal and the administration fees which are paid quarterly, we have:

$$285{,}850 = 200 \cdot PVIFA_{120,N} + 300{,}000 \cdot (1 + 0.015)^{120} \cdot (1 + R)^{-120}.$$

The effective interest rate will then be 1.5733 % per quarter, or 6.4 % p.a. Therefore we see that is it cheaper to have the interest payments deferred until maturity and added to the principal for each coupon period.

Loans with equal payment of principal and interest (annuity)
Loans that are amortized over a number of time periods, *with equal payments every time period*, are similar to annuities. This loan structure is often used in consumer repayment mortgages or in unsecured small business bank loans. If the interest rate is fixed, the equilibrium equation for a loan with equal annual payments of principal and interest can be written as:

$$NP_0 = \text{Annuity payment} \cdot PVIFA_{R,N}$$

where

NP_0	= net proceeds.
Annuity payment	= equal payment per time period.
N	= lifetime of the loan in time periods.
R	= effective interest rate per time period.

Figure 10.1 gives a graphical illustration for this type of loan with equal payments, where payments are divided into interest and installments.

Interest payments per time period decrease due to the gradual amortization of the loan amount. Because installment payments per time period are constant, the amount of money going to principal amortization increases over time.

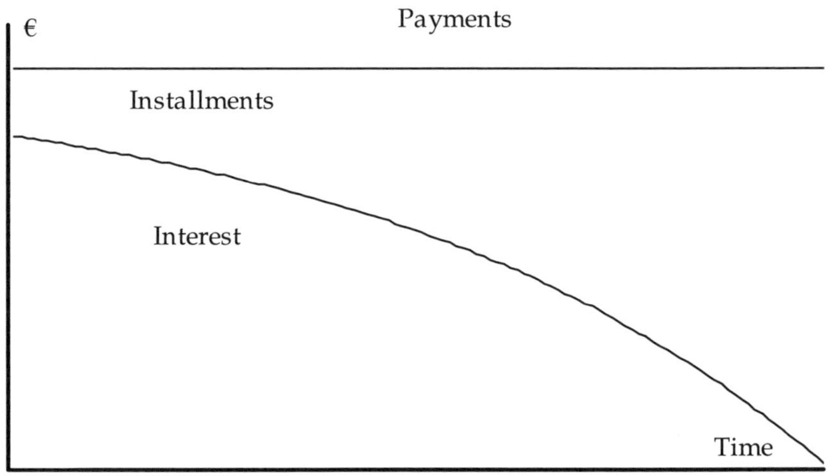

Figure 10.1 Installments and interest schedule

The equal payments per time period will almost always be stated in nominal prices before tax. Because most interest payments are tax-deductible, we may wish to calculate net payments after tax. Since they will no longer be constant we cannot use the previous equation, but will have to utilize the general formula:

$$NP_0 = \sum_{t=1}^{N} CF_t \cdot (1+R)^{-t}$$

where

NP_0	= net proceeds after tax.
CF_t	= payment after tax at time t.
N	= lifetime of the loan in time periods.
R	= the effective interest rate per time period after tax.

Example 10.2

We will use the data from Example 10.1 and apply it to a loan with equal payments of principal and interest. The equal payment per time period is calculated as an annuity based on the principal, the lifetime of the loan, and the nominal interest rate per time period. There is also a €200 administration fee:

$$\text{Payment} = \boldsymbol{300{,}000 \cdot PVIFA^{-1}_{120,1,5\%} + 200} = €5{,}605.56 \text{ per quarter.}$$

The equilibrium equation to calculate the yield to maturity will be:

$$285{,}850 = 5{,}605.56 \cdot \text{PVIFA}_{120,\,R}.$$

$$\text{PVIFA}_{120,\,R} = \frac{285{,}850}{5{,}605.56} = 50.994013\,.$$

Calculating on the basis of this, we have: R = 1.7023 % per quarter, or 6.99 % p.a. So, we see that the effective interest rate in this example will be 0.99 % higher p.a. than the nominal interest rate.

The following table shows the details of installments, interest and remaining debt, for the first five time periods.

Time period	Payment	Interest	Installment	Remaining debt
0				€300,000
1	€5,406	€4,500	€906	€299,094
2	€5,406	€4,486	€920	€298,175
3	€5,406	€4,473	€933	€297,242
4	€5,406	€4,459	€947	€296,295
5	€5,406	€4,444	€961	€295,334

Loans with installment-free periods (grace periods)

Loans can be structured to include periods with no installments. This will often take place during the first periods, where cash flow constraints can be tightest, but the installment-free periods may also take place at other times. A general formula for calculating the effective interest rate cannot be made, as it depends on exactly when the installment-free periods occur throughout the lifetime of the loan. Figure 10.2 illustrates how a payment schedule might look for a loan when installments are not paid at the outset.

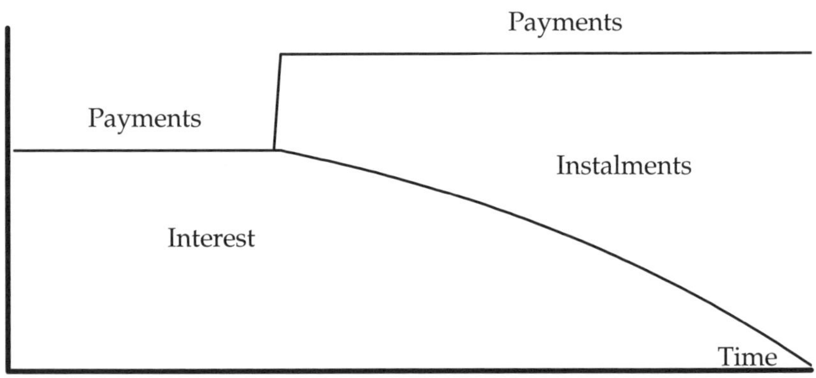

Figure 10.2 Payments, installments, and interest

Figure 10.2 shows payments, installments, and interest for a loan with grace periods, where the grace periods occur at the beginning of the loan.

Below is another possible type of loan, where the repayment schedule alternates between installment-free periods to periods with instalments and is then followed by final amortization of the loan. This illustrates the way in which loans can be structured between lender and borrower according to individual specific needs.

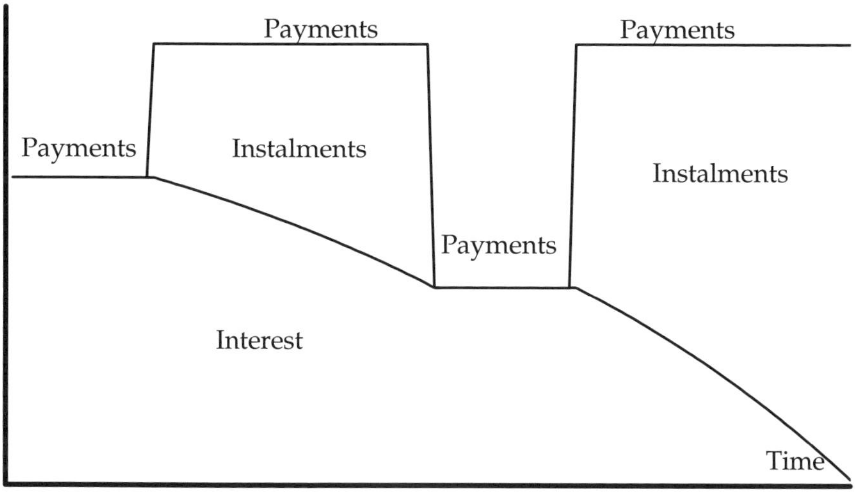

Figure 10.3 Sequence of payments, installments, and interest

Figure 10.3 show the sequence of payments, installments, and interest for an installment-free loan with the installment-free periods distributed over the lifetime of the loan.

In the agreed-upon schedule for amortization, payments are the same size during periods with installments, regardless of where the installment-free periods are placed. These payments are calculated with equal-sized payments (annuities), on the basis of the nominal interest rate, with a lifetime which corresponds to the number of time periods with installments.

$$\text{Payment}_{\text{Installment period}} = \text{P} \cdot \text{PVIFA}_{\text{N,R}}^{-1}$$

where

P is the principal of the loan.
N is the number of time periods with instalments.
R is the nominal interest rate per time period of the loan.

The payment in the installment-free periods depends on where they are placed. Interest payments during this period depend on the outstanding loan amount.

Example 10.3
We will use the data from Example 6.1. However, we will now assume a 30-year loan with equal payments, including 10 years of installment-free periods occurring at various times throughout the loan schedule.

We will first analyze the loan with installment-free periods occurring at the beginning of the loan. The payment per time period is calculated on the basis of the principal, the number of time periods, the nominal interest rate per time period, and the €200 administration fees. Installment-free periods will include the interest and administration fee only, whereas the payments during instalment periods will include amortization also:

$$\text{Payment}_{\text{Installment-free period}} = 300{,}000 \cdot 0.015 + 200 = €4{,}700 \text{ per quarter.}$$

$$\text{Payment}_{\text{Installment period}} = \boldsymbol{300{,}000 \cdot PVIFA_{80,1.5\%}^{-1} + 200} = €6{,}664.50 \text{ per quarter.}$$

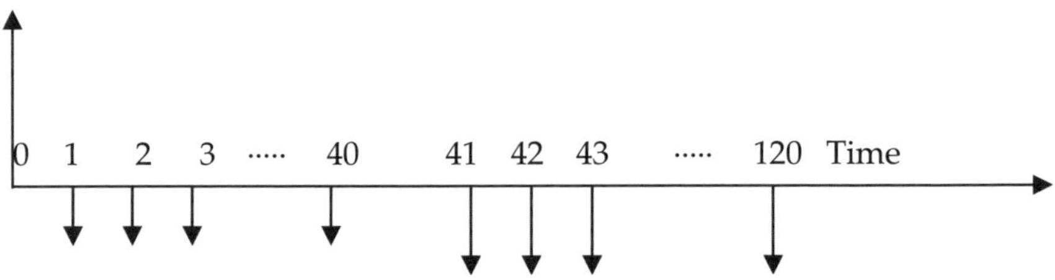

Figure 10.4 Payments on an installment-free loan over 120 time periods with 40 installment-free periods in the beginning of the lifetime of the loan

The equilibrium between net proceeds and the discounted value of future cash flows will be:

$$285{,}850 = 4{,}700 \cdot \text{PVIFA}_{40,\text{R}} + 6{,}646.50 \cdot \text{PVIFA}_{80,\text{R}} \cdot (1+\text{R})^{-40}.$$

The first 40 quarterly time periods (where only interest is paid) will be discounted to time 0 as an annuity. The next 80 time periods where both interest and installments are paid are first discounted back to time t=40 as an annuity, then discounted back to time 0 as one total amount. Using a spreadsheet, we find R = 1.6818 % per quarter, or 6.9 % p.a. This means that the true interest rate in this example will be 0.9 % higher per year than the nominal interest rate.

If the placement of the installment-free periods is changed to begin with 5 installment-free years, followed by 10 years with installments, then another 5 installment-free years, and finally 10 years with installments, we have the payment sequence shown in Figure 10.3 above.

- 20 time periods paying interest only.
- 40 time periods paying interest plus instalments.
- 20 time periods paying interest only.
- 40 time periods paying interest plus instalments.

The calculations are somewhat more difficult, because the lifetime of the loan is now divided into 4 periods.

In order to determine the size of payments in the second installment-free period, it is necessary to know how much remaining debt there will be after the first 60 time periods have ended. This makes the calculation even more difficult; in such cases, we recommend using the solver add-in in Excel or else specialized financial tools. The effective interest rate per quarter is found to be 1.6953 %, or 6.96 % p.a.

Loans with equal payments of principal

A loan with equal payments of principal would have the loan principal amortized over a number of time periods, *with equal installments during every time period.* Interest decreases as the loan principal is amortized and since installments are constant, the total payment will decrease over time.

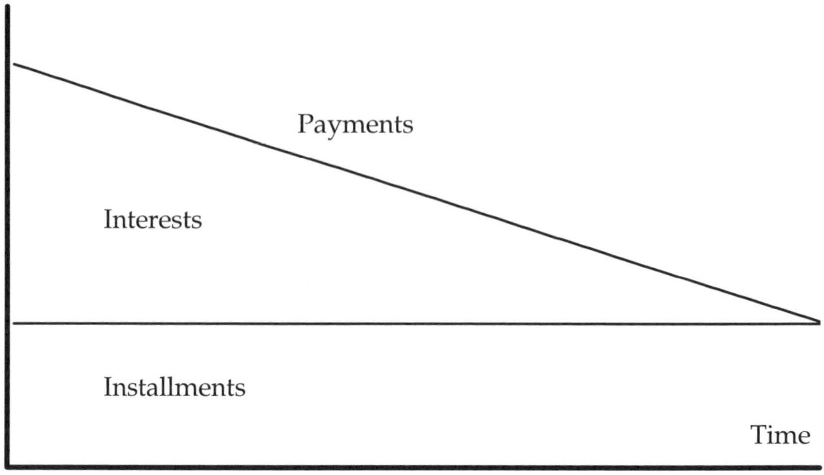

Figure 10.5 Sequence of payments, installments, and interest

If the loan has a fixed interest rate, we can calculate the effective yield of the loan by using:

$$NP_0 = \sum_{t=1}^{N} CF_t \cdot (1+R)^{-t} \ .$$

In practice, this calculation is found by using a financial calculator or spreadsheet[1].

Example 10.4
We will use the data from Example 10.1 again, but we will now assume a loan with equal payments of principal. Installments per time period will

[1] The general formula to determine the effective interest rate a loan with equal payments of principal is:

$$\text{Price} = \frac{R_{nom}}{R} + \frac{1}{N} \cdot (1 - \frac{R_{nom}}{R}) \cdot PVIFA_{N,R} \ .$$

be calculated as follows: $\frac{300,000}{120}$ = €2,500. The €200 administration fees and interest are added to this, so the effective interest rate under these conditions will be 1.7414 % per time period, or 7.15 % p.a. This loan's effective interest rate is therefore slightly higher than that of a similar loan having equal payments of principal and interest. This is the case despite the fact that the total accumulated payments on the loan with equal payments of principal and interest will be €648,667, compared to only €572,250 on the loan with equal payments of principal.

This paradox is caused by the fact that payments on the loan with equal payments of principal during the first time periods are almost 30 % higher than payments on the loan with equal, annuity payments of principal and interest. Also, payments occurring nearer to the present have a greater net present value weight than payments occurring farther into the future once discounting is done. Only after 43 to 44 time periods do payments on the two loans reach the same level; until then, payments on the loan with equal payments of principal are larger than payments on loans with equal, annuity payments of principal and interest. The following table shows developments in payments, installments, interest and the remaining debt for the first five time periods:

Time Period	Payments	Installments	Interest	Debt Outstanding
0				€300,000
1	€7,000	€2,500	€4,500	€297,500
2	€6,963	€2,500	€4,463	€295,000
3	€6,925	€2,500	€4,425	€292,500
4	€6,888	€2,500	€4,388	€290,000
5	€6,850	€2,500	€4,350	€287,500

Price = net proceeds per €1 face value.
R_{nom} = nominal interest rate per time period.
R = effective interest rate per time period.
N = number of time periods.

Both loans have advantages and disadvantages: *The advantage of the loan with equal, annuity payments of principal and interest* is that initial payments are lower than with a loan having equal payments of principal. Furthermore, a significant portion of the early payments is comprised of interest, which in most cases is tax-deductible. Therefore, after-tax payments for a loan with equal, annuity payments of principal and interest will be significantly less than a loan with equal payments of principal.

The disadvantages of this type loan however, are that the before-tax payments remain constant over the full lifespan of the loan and that it takes a long time before the debt is amortized significantly.

The advantage of a loan with equal payments of principal is that the debt is amortized by the same amount in every time period over the lifetime of the loan. The initial time periods reduce the outstanding debt as much as the last ones do. Another advantage is that payments become less and less over time.

The disadvantage of this type of loan is that the payments are relatively large in the initial periods. Furthermore, the tax advantage is relatively smaller because interest makes up a smaller portion of the initial payments.

Mixing of loans

In order to balance advantages and disadvantages of the different loan types, a *mix* is sometimes used. In this case, the principal is divided into parts. *One part of the loan has equal payments of principal and interest, while the other part has equal payments of principal.* In this way, the repayment schedule provides a compromise between the two types of loans.

Calculations on mixed loans are difficult to perform unless we use computer programs and spreadsheets. The two loans must be treated separately because we cannot calculate the effective interest rate as a weighted average of the two loan types' effective interest rate. The payment schedules for each type must be listed and the calculations made from there.

Figure 10.6 show payments of interest and installments for a mixed loan where 60 % of the periods have equal payments of principal and interest, and 40 % have equal payments of principal.

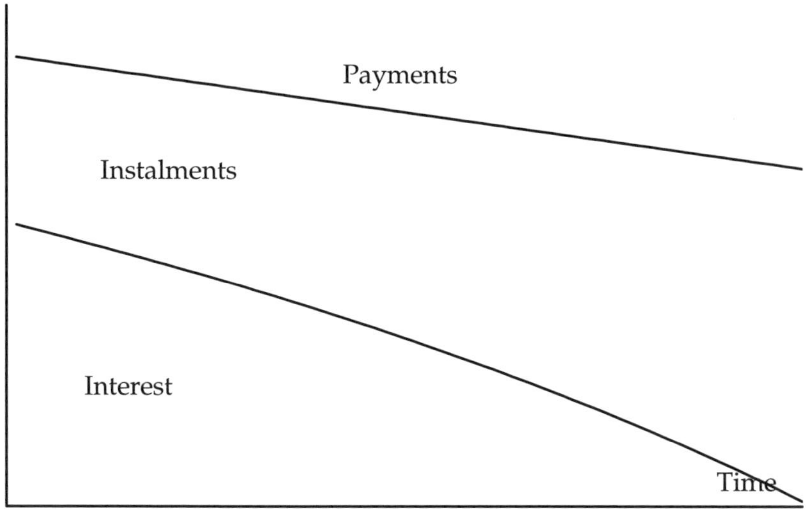

Figure 10.6 Payments, installments, and interest for a mixed loan

Example 10.5
Mr. Brown's purchase of a home is currently structured with a mixed loan having 60 % equal payments of principal and interest, and 40 % equal payments of principal. The loan's price, lifespan, costs, and fees are the same as those given in Example 10.1. The principal amount of €300,000 will now be divided into a loan of €180,000 with equal payments of principal and interest, and one of €120,000 with equal payments of principal.

The effective interest is 1.7164 % per time period, or 7.04 % p.a. As expected, since this is a mixed loan, its interest rate falls between that of a loan having equal payments of principal and interest and one having equal payments of principal.

The payments, interest, and debt outstanding over the first five time periods are illustrated below:

Time Period	Payments	Instalments	Interest	Debt Outstanding
0				€300,000
1	€6,043	€1,543	€4,500	€298,457
2	€6,028	€1,551	€4,477	€296,905
3	€6,013	€1,559	€4,454	€295,345
4	€5,998	€1,568	€4,430	€293,777
5	€5,983	€1,576	€4,407	€292,201

The following table provides an overview of the effective interest rate per quarter and per year for each of the different loan types discussed in Examples 10.1 to 10.5:

Effective interest rate in %	Per Quarter	Per Year
Bullet loan with payments of interest	1.66 %	6.80 %
Bullet loan with compounding of interest	1.57 %	6.44 %
Loan with equal payment of principal and interest	1.70 %	6.99 %
Installment-free loan 1	1.68 %	6.90 %
Installment-free loan 2	1.70 %	6.96 %
Loan with equal payments of principal	1.74 %	7.15 %
Mixed loan	1.72 %	7.04 %

Overdraft facility

An *overdraft facility*, or line of credit, is probably the most widely used form of financing. It allows for fluctuations in a company's liquidity. Because it gives the company the right, but not the obligation to borrow, the overdraft facility is used to cover needs. During periods where a company has surplus liquidity, the overdraft facility is replenished, and the amount outstanding reduces.

Borrowers are attracted to overdraft facilities because they provide financing at relatively low costs. Also, the borrower is not asked to forecast the exact amount and duration of his borrowing, but simply to accept a maximum limit. Overdraft interest is charged only on the actual daily debit balance outstanding, and the repayment of borrowing carries no penalty. These aspects, also, provide an attractive flexibility.

Interest on the overdraft facility typically accrues on a monthly or quarterly basis according to the balance outstanding at any given time. To calculate the effective cost of capital on an overdraft facility, we include other costs and fees, in addition to the interest itself. Two types of costs are typical in this respect:

1. One-time costs.
2. Current costs and fees.

One-time costs typically include an establishment fee, duty stamp, registration fee for collateral, etc. Current costs and fees, meanwhile, include interest and any service fees, plus a possible commission fee on the overdraft facility's maximum limit.

An overdraft facility rarely has a fixed lifetime. In some cases, overdrafts are established with a relatively short lifetime, but usually the agreement can be extended automatically without any extra costs. Therefore the overdraft facility can be seen as a revolving right to borrow.

Interest rates on overdraft facilities are not fixed in advance, but float in accordance with market interest rates. Charges for individual borrowers may vary according to the borrower's credit risk, size, or market strength, etc.

Supplier or trade credits

The simplest way for a company to obtain short-term financing is to delay payment for goods received. *Supplier or trade credits are therefore a commonly used form of financing.* The availability and conditions of supplier and trade credits are highly dependent upon the relationship between seller and buyer. Supplier and trade credit can involve different cost elements such as:

1. Lost cash discounts.
2. Costs of establishing the loan documents.

3. Current administration costs and fees.

The effective interest rate of supplier credit can be calculated by equating net proceeds with the discounted value of future cash flows. The net proceeds are the price of the good or service, minus potential cash discounts, where cash discounts represent the alternative price that would have been paid at the time of purchase. The right side of the equilibrium equation includes any costs to establish the credit, payment for the good or service, and potential administration costs. All of these are discounted back to the time of purchase at the effective interest rate.

In business-to-business relationships, it is common for the buyer to choose between a cash discount and a certain period of credit. In these cases, there are typically no establishment fees. The effective interest rate of the supplier credit can be calculated directly as:

$$\text{Price} - \text{cash discount} = \text{Price} \cdot (1 + \text{R})^{-1},$$

which can be re-written as:

$$R = \frac{\textit{Cash discount}}{\textit{Price - Cash discount}}.$$

The effective interest rate which we calculate here covers the time interval between when a cash payment is made and when payment would be made according to supplier credit. To calculate a supplier credit's effective interest rate per year, we would use:

$$R_{p.a.} = (1+R)^{\frac{360}{Daysofcredit}} - 1.$$

Example 10.6
A supplier offers a 1.5 % cash discount with 5 day's credit. Alternatively, credit is given for the current month plus 30 days, which on average amounts to 45 days. Therefore the average credit time, if credit is accepted, amounts to 40 days (i.e., 45 days minus 5 days).

For simplicity, if we assume that the price of the good or service is €100, we would receive a €1.50 discount. We can calculate the true 40-day interest rate from this:

$$R = \frac{1.5}{100-1.5} = 0.015228\,.$$

The 40 days credit time is equal to one-ninth of a year. Therefore, the annual true interest rate will be:

$$R_{p.a.} = (1 + 0.015228)^9 - 1 = 0.1457 \text{ or } 14.57\ \% \text{ p.a.}$$

Another type of credit is a 12-month interest-free account. This is typically seen in retail shops, where the customer normally does not have the opportunity to obtain cash discounts. In return for the credit, the customer will typically need to pay an establishment fee, and perhaps also some montly administrative costs. The effective interest rate per month can be calculated from the equilibrium equation:

$$\text{Price} = \text{establishment costs} + \sum_{t=1}^{N} (\mathit{instalments} + \text{fees.})_t \cdot (1+R)^{-t}\,.$$

The effective interest rate per year can then be found by using the formula for interest rate computation:

$$R_{p.a.} = (1 + R)^{12} - 1.$$

Example 10.7

A designer furniture shop offers to finance the purchase of exclusive furniture costing €10,005 with a 12 or 24-month interest-free account. It requires a 10 % down payment at the time of purchase, plus administration fees of €25 per month; there is also an establishment fee of €275. Monthly payments, including administration fees, are calculated at €850 with a 12-month credit, and at €437 with a 24-month credit. The respective effective interest rate for the 12 and 24-month credit offers can now be calculated:

$$\text{Price} - \text{down payment} = \text{establishment fee} + \text{payment} \cdot PVIFA_{N,R}.$$

The calculation for the 12-month credit will be:

$$10{,}005 - (10{,}005 \cdot 0.10) = 275 + 850 \cdot \text{PVIFA}_{12,R}.$$

which gives an effective interest rate of 0.9115 % per month, or 11.50 % p.a.

Over the 24 months, the calculation will be:

$$10{,}005 - (10{,}005 \cdot 0.10) = 275 + 437 \cdot \text{PVIFA}_{24,R,}$$

which gives an effective interest rate of 0.7025 % per month, or 8.76 % p.a.

Leasing

Leasing involves an arrangement whereby one party (the 'lessor') purchases and owns an item of equipment, and allows another party (the 'lessee') to use it. The lessee then makes periodic payments, known as rentals, to the lessor over the life of the lease. The lease may be structured so that adequate rentals are paid to the lessor over an initial period, which lets him recover the purchase price and financing costs, plus earn a profit margin. At the end of the lease term, the lessee may receive most of the proceeds resulting from any sale of the asset. This situation is different from operating leases, where the lessee might or might not commit to a number of rental periods which fully buys out the lessor.

The leasing agreement, which normally has a shorter span than the economic lifetime of the equipment, determines how much the company must pay per month for the rental. This rental cost will often be expressed as a percentage of the equipment's purchase price.

The most important reason why a company leases equipment is because it can avoid paying the entire purchase price all at once. Instead, it can pay for it over a longer period, which may be advantageous for liquidity reasons.

One motivation for leasing which is often quoted in connection with leasing agreements is that it offers a tax advantage. This can be true in some countries where leasing arrangements receive special tax advantages, but in general this is not necessarily the case. For instance, if we consider the tax advantages of depreciation (which requires an equipment purchase), purchasing will be more advantageous than leasing.

At the expiration of the leasing period, the equipment belongs to the leasing company. In some cases it can be leased again, normally for a significantly reduced lease payment. In other cases, the lessee company may have right of first refusal to purchase the equipment at a preset price.

Example 10.8
A company is about to buy a new production facility for €240,000. The new equipment has an anticipated five-year useful life, after which it has no scrap value and must be replaced.. The company can either buy the plant or lease it at a predetermined monthly lease payment of 2.2 % of the original purchase price. If the production plant is purchased, the company will use straight-line depreciation over the 5-year life. It employs a 10 % cost of capital before tax and expects an annual tax rate of 34 % over the next 5 years.

The lease payment per month before tax is:

$$240{,}000 \cdot 0.022 = €5{,}280.$$

To evaluate whether the company should buy or lease the plant, we can calculate the net present value and the effective interest rate.

Using a year as the time period
If the time period is fixed at one year, all cash inflows and outflows during the year will be treated as if they occured on the last day of that year. For the leasing agreement, this gives an annual payment of:

$$5{,}280 \cdot 12 = €63{,}360.$$

The net present value of this will be:

$$NPV_{0,\,leasing} = -63{,}360 \cdot PVIFA_{5,\,10\,\%} = -€240{,}184.45.$$

The effective interest rate before tax of the lease agreement can now be determined:

$$240{,}000 = 63{,}360 \cdot \text{PVIFA}_{5,\,R'}$$

which gives an effective interest rate of 10.03 % p.a.

Comparing this 10.03 % effective interest rate to the company's 10 % cost of capital, we see that the financial benefit of buying versus leasing the plant is almost negligible. The difference in the net present value of the two options is €184.45 (on a purchase of €240,000), and the difference of the effective interest rate for the two options is 0.03 % p.a.

Using a month as the time period

If the leasing time period is fixed on a monthly basis instead, the cost of capital per month will be:

$$R_{month} = (\sqrt[12]{1.1} - 1) \cdot 100 = 0.7974\% .$$

The lease payment can now be thought of as a prepaid annuity:

$$\text{Present value} = -5{,}280 - 5{,}280 \cdot \text{PVIFA}_{59\rceil 0.7974} = -€253{,}005.$$

The effective interest rate per month can be determined as:

$$240{,}000 = 5{,}280 + 5{,}280 \cdot \text{PVIFA}_{59,\,R}.$$

The effective interest rate per month before tax is then 0.9958 % and 12.63 % p.a. before tax. The difference between a purchase and leasing is therefore larger when the time period is set to be shorter; purchasing now looks somewhat more advantageous.

After-tax

When tax considerations are included, we see a somewhat different situation. The lease agreement requires a monthly payment of €5,280, so the question is, how to deal with the reduction in tax:

- Should the tax reduction be subtracted from the monthly payments?
- Should it be regarded as one total reduction occurring at the end of the year?
- Or should it be regarded as a reduction occurring in the beginning of the following year?

In the following calculations we have chosen to assume that the tax reduction will occur at the end of the year.

The annual lease payment is calculated by discounting the monthly payments forward to the end of the year, using the company's after-tax cost of capital. The tax reduction should be deducted from the annual lease payment as follows:

$$\text{Payment per month} \cdot 12 \cdot \text{tax percentage}$$

$$\text{Tax reduction per year} = 5{,}280 \cdot 12 \cdot 0.34 = €21{,}542.40.$$

The total annual payment is calculated as the end value of a prepaid annuity of 12 time periods. First, we calculate the after-tax cost of capital per month:

$$R_{month} = \sqrt[12]{(1 + 0.066)} - 1 = 0.00534032 \text{ or } 0.5340\ \%.$$

The total annual lease payment after tax can now be calculated as:

$$\text{Payment}_{year} = \text{Payment}_{month} \cdot \text{FVIFA}_{12,0,534\ \%} \cdot 1.0053 - 21{,}542.40$$
$$= €44{,}060.60.$$

The net present value of the lease agreement can now be calculated as:

$$\text{NPV}_{0,leasing} = -44{,}060.60 \cdot \text{PVIFA}_{5,\ 6,6\ \%} = -€184{,}608.62.$$

If the company chooses to buy the plant instead, it must invest €240,000. However, this amount will be reduced by the net present value of the tax reductions caused by depreciation. The plant will use straight-line depreciation over 5 years, which gives an annual depreciation of €48,000. At a tax rate of 34 %, this will give an annual reduction of 40,000 · 0.34 = €16,320. The net present value of the purchase can now be calculated as:

$$NPV_{0,purchase} = -240{,}000 + 16{,}320 \cdot PVIFA_{5,\,6.6\,\%} = -€172{,}362.00.$$

From a purely financial evaluation, buying still looks like the best alternative. However, the difference of €12,246.62 (or 6.63 %), is very small. Therefore, other considerations such as maintenance costs, services, etc. may influence the decision of whether to buy or lease.

Example 10.9
Miss Johnson is interested in buying a new Harley Davidson motorcycle. She has been offered financing alternatives by the dealership as follows:

1. Cash payment. The motorcycle will cost €5,695, plus €400 in delivery charges.
2. A 12-month interest-free account. This offer entails €400 in delivery costs, plus a €240 fee to establish the account.
3. A 33-month lease contract with monthly payments (in advance) of €214, after which the bike can be bought for €1. This offer entails a €240 fee to establish the lease contract, plus a one-month advance payment deposit which will be deducted from the lease payment.

Miss Johnson has the required cash on hand of €6,095 (€5,695 + €400) and could buy the motorcycle outright, but she is considering financing the purchase instead. She therefore wishes to compare the potential financing alternatives with this cash amount. Before she makes her decision, she consults her bank, which gives her an additional offer as follows:

Purpose of loan	Purchase of motorcycle
Borrowing amount	€2,000 to €40,000
Period of loan	3 - 72 months
Costs: Establishment fee Monthly account fee Administration fee	 2 % of the borrowed amount €12 Free if payments are done electronically, otherwise €13 per transaction
Public duties	Duty stamp for the government if the loan exceeds €16,667
Interest	1.99 % per month The interest rate is fixed over the life of the loan

For each of the three non-cash alternatives given above, we can calculate how much Miss Johnson would pay in down payment and monthly payments. This will allow us to determine the effective interest rate for each alternative. The bank loan would be repaid in equal payments at the end of each month, whereas the financing alternatives given by the store are month-ahead annuities.

	Bank	Harley Davidson Dealer	
		12 months interest-free	Lease contract
Interest rate per month	1.99 %		
Loan	€6,000		
Establishment	€120		
Net proceeds	€5,880		
Down payment	€215	€640	€454
Monthly payment	€316.87	€474.58	€214
Fee per month	€12		
Total costs per month	€328.87	€474.58	€214
Effective monthly interest rate	2.50 %	0.79 %	1.30 %
Effective interest rate p.a.	**34.53 %**	**9.94 %**	**16.84 %**

Analysis of bank loan financing

The bank has offered a 24-month loan of €6,000, from which we deduct a €120 establishment fee. This leaves net proceeds of €5,880, so Miss Johnson will have to finance the remaining €215 herself. The monthly payment to the bank is calculated as follows:

$$\text{Payment} = 6{,}000 \cdot \text{PVIFA}_{24,1,99\,\%}{}^{-1} = €316.87.$$

There is also a monthly fee of €12 which is added to the monthly payment, giving a payment to the bank of €328.87 per month. Thus, the equilibrium equation will now be:

$$5{,}880 = 328.87 \cdot \text{PVIFA}_{24,\,R}.$$

The effective interest rate is therefore 34.53 % p.a.

Analysis of 12-month interest-free account

In this case, Miss Johnson will pay for the account's delivery and establishment costs, which will total €640. After that, the prepaid monthly payments will be $\frac{5.695}{12}$ = €474.58. The equilibrium equation will therefore yield:

$$5{,}695 = 240 + 474.58 \cdot \text{PVIFA}_{12,\,R} \cdot (1+R).$$

This implies an effective interest rate of 16.84 % p.a.

33-Month Lease Agreement Analysis

In this case, Miss Johnson will pay €240 for the establishment of the lease contract and a deposit of €214. Delivery is free when leasing, so her first payment will total €454. The monthly lease payment is €214, which covers the month in advance. Miss Johnson therefore has to make lease payments for 32 months, since the last payment is covered by the deposit. The equilibrium equation will be:

$$6{,}095 = 214 \cdot \text{PVIFA}_{32,\,R} \cdot (1+R) + 454.$$

So, the effective interest rate is 9.94 % p.a.

The effective interest rate for each of the three alternatives can be seen in the table above. The cheapest alternative is the 12-month interest-free account, with an effective interest rate of 9.94 % p.a. The bank is the most expensive alternative, at 34.53 % p.a.

CHAPTER 11

Business and Financial Risk

Tools for Optimizing the Financial Structure

A fundamental principle in investment theory is that the investor will execute investment strategies only where the perceived risk is justified by the required return on invested capital. A classic correlation between the required return on investment and the perceived risk is the so-called capital market line:

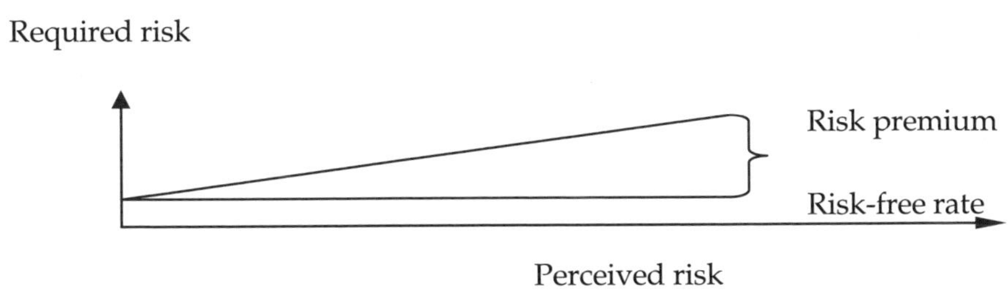

Figure 11.1 Capital market line

The risk-free rate is typically equated with the rate of the return on government (treasury) bonds issued by countries whose repayment likeliness is nearly risk-free as determined by international rating agencies. This rate is an estimated value because government bonds are typically standing loans, made and refinanced, while project financing usually involves a repayment scheme whose instalment payments are made at consistent intervals. Also, in most cases the time horizon on government bonds may differ from the specific financing for a particular investment. However, for practical purposes we can accept this approximation.

A risk premium should be added to the risk-free rate as compensation for the perceived risk on a lender's future repayment cash flows. A number of comprehensive mathematical models exist for estimating this "unavoidable" risk; a classical tool is the Capital Asset Pricing Model (CAPM) for listed companies. In this book we work with a practical framework for closely held companies which estimates the risks associated with the assets to be financed. In this case, we can establish a measure for the risk premium by analyzing its two components:

1) Financial risk.
2) Business risk.

To increase shareholder value, our investment strategies should be placed on or above the capital market line so that our return compensates us for the risk we are taking on – the so-called hurdle rate. This will lead to an increased shareholder value, as the return on investment will then exceed the applicable discount rate. If we pursue investment strategies which lie below the capital market line, shareholder value will be reduced because the rate of return is no longer commensurate with risk exposure. For example, this could be the case if the company were to undertake potentially high-yielding investments containing a disproportionately high risk profile.

But the investment risk is not an absolute which cannot change; the decision-maker can look for strategic ways to reduce investment risk and in many cases, a given strategic objective can be achieved in different ways, each bearing different risks. If the main goal of the investment is for example market access this strategic objective can be achieved in a variety of different ways, including:

- Organic expansion (self-financed growth built on a company's own organizational resources).
- Licensing.
- Franchising.
- Strategic alliances.
- Joint ventures.

- Acquisition (for example, horizontal or vertical integration).
- Creating a fully-owned subsidiary.

A company's level of business risk tends to increase as it moves directionally from organic expansion towards establishing a 100 % owned subsidiary. Consequently, the expected advantages of higher growth and greater rate of return must also be present as a reward for the increased risk.

It is therefore important for companies to consider strategic alternatives in the investment decisions they make, as considerable shareholder value will be at stake.

Additional strategic management approaches which lead to rates of return on or above the capital market line can be applied when choosing investment structures. Two examples are given below:

1. External situations: The company can seek to identify, use, and protect business areas which yield higher rates of return when there is growth potential, barriers to entry, or protected markets such as a monopoly, oligopoly, etc.
2. Internal resources: The company can maintain focus on core competencies in order to use and protect its competitive advantages.

Next, we will define financial and business risk and discuss how an understanding of these concepts can help a company improve its financing structures. Finally, we will look at refinancing as a management tool.

Financial Risk – Debt/Equity

Financial risk is determined by a company's capital structure – that is, how much debt it holds in relation to its equity. An increase in the debt/equity ratio drives an increase in financial risk, mainly because debt has a repayment schedule. This requirement to repay creates a pressure to comply with the ongoing financial obligation, regardless of business developments. An increase in financial risk will therefore lead to an increase in risk premium.

The ratio between equity and debt is a key variable when deciding upon the optimal capital structure. To the company, equity can be seen as a financial resource to be injected which secures a maximum return to shareholders and provides an adequate security for the debt. Debt is attractive to the company as long as its marginal price is lower than the rate of return on assets (ROA). This relationship between the marginal price of debt and ROA is called the interest rate margin. It is calculated as ROA minus the average interest rate on debt. As long as the interest rate margin is positive, it will lead to a continued increase in return on equity (ROE), and increasing debt-to-equity in this way is called financial gearing. A high financial gearing means the company holds a large amount of debt compared to equity.

The other side of increasing debt-to-equity is that the company's financial risk will increase. Therefore, we would typically see the marginal price of debt rise in line with the increase of total debt. This means that the benefits from debt financing (interest rate margin) decrease with the amount borrowed, until the interest rate margin has been exhausted.

Example 11.1
Consider two companies, with different financial structures as illustrated:

	X	Y
Equity	750,000	250,000
Debt	250,000	750,000
Total capital/liabilities	1,000,000	1,000,000

The operational results for the two companies are as follows:

	X	Y
Earnings before financial costs (interest) (EBIT)	120,000	120,000
Financial costs (interest)	25,000	75,000
Profit after financial costs (interest)	95,000	45,000

Return on Assets (ROA)	12.0 %	12.0 %
Return on Equity (ROE)	12.6 %	18.0 %

For both companies, the earnings before the interest (EBI) are €120,000, and the return on assets (ROA) is therefore 12 %. With an average rate of interest on debt of 10 %, the financial costs of Companies X and Y would be €25,000 and €75,000, respectively. Thus, the earnings after interest are €95,000 for Company X and €45,000 for Company Y. This yields a return on equity (ROE) of 12.6 % for Company X and 18 % for Company Y.

We see that Company Y's marginal price of debt is less than its ROA – that is, 10 % is less than 12 %. As long as this relationship holds true, the companies can improve ROE by sourcing larger amounts of debt (i.e., gearing its financial structure). As a result of greater debt, Company Y's ROE is better than Company X's, even though Company Y has higher financial costs.

On the other hand, Company Y is significantly more vulnerable to adverse business conditions. Even if it suffers a decline in earnings it must still meet its debt service requirements, which are higher than Company X's. Also, Company Y's liquidity requirements, as specified in its debt repayment schedule might well come under severe financial stress in such a business downturn. It might also prove more difficult for Company Y to source the additional necessary financing in this situation than it would be for Company X, which holds much lower debt. These factors mean that Company Y's financial risk (gearing) will be higher than that of Company X.

Banks and financial institutions willing to lend out money to a project or a company assess the key risks associated with the borrower's risk of default and determining what the financial consequences will be if the borrower experiences trouble. Therefore, the marginal price of debt typically increases as the financial gearing goes up because the company's ability to provide coverage security is reduced at the same time as the strain on cash flow from debt servicing is increased.

The company must therefore decide on a level of debt which, on the one hand, ensures maximum shareholder value, but, on the other, does not increase financial risk beyond a level where the return on invested capital does not compensate it sufficiently for the price (or, risk) at the capital market line.

Here again, the decisions a company makes about its financial structure represent a strategic tool it can use to manage financial risk. Seen from the company's point of view, financial risk increases as debt places more constraints on liquidity and assets. With the key forms of financing listed below, financial risk increases from left to right:

Equity
Subordinated loan capital
Mezzanine capital
Subordinated loan
Secured loan

We have discussed equity already. Mezzanine capital is debt financing provided by shareholders or external mezzanine finance institutions. Typically, the debt's terms are based on some form of participation in the project or company profits: If things turn out well, there is an upside to share; if they do not, the upside is limited. In exchange, the repayment schedule has a low interest rate and instalments which depend on the company's cash flows. Mezzanine financing typically does not require mortgages, security, or the like. It is therefore considered close to being equity and contributes to the solidity of the company.

Subordinated loans have a secondary priority with regard to security and mortgage, which means that in a bankruptcy situation they would be repaid only once senior debt is satisfied. Subordinated loads are often structured with more flexible repayment terms than ordinary, secured loans.

Business and Project Risk

From a practical point of view, business and project risk can be determined by:

1. The company's industry and.
2. Its cost structure.

A relatively high business risk naturally increases the uncertainty of estimated future cash flows and possible outcome scenarios. Business risk can be assessed by analyzing the following factors:

- Demand uncertainty (product life cycle etc).
- Price fluctuations and availability of input factors (e.g. supplier strength).
- Growth drivers (expansion opportunities/ability).
- Sales price volatility (price setting/market forms).
- Competitive rivalry/market's desirability (Porter's five forces).
- The company's position among competitors.
- The opportunities and threats in the outside world (PESTEL).

The business risk for a given industry is typically linked to the industry's market conditions. These are comprised of such things as cyclical sensitivity, technology, competitive strategy, and the company's market position. A start-up company in a highly competitive arena will have considerably more business risk than a large company which is well-positioned, diversified, and operates in a stable market.

The business and project risk related to the company's cost structure is determined by the relationship between fixed and variable costs, or the so-called operational leverage. All things being equal, a capital-intensive company with high fixed costs will have a greater business risk than one with mostly variable costs because an unexpected downturn will impact its cash flow more. Thus, there is typically a trade-off between using operating leverage to obtain cost advantages at high production volumes and reducing business risk by choosing a more variable cost structure.

An assessment of business risk must therefore analyze the company's cost structure, and understand the degree of operating risk, perhaps through a break-even analysis. The break-even analysis should specifically consider the risk related to volume changes within the given project or company.

The Combination of Business Risk and Financial Risk

Financial structuring should evaluate the match between business risk and financial risk. This way, an unwise combination of high business risk and high financial risk can be avoided, as in the case of highly leveraged debt financing at a biotechnology start-up. As a general rule, projects with higher business risk should implement financial structures with lower financial risk. This can be done by opting for proportionately more equity and share capital than debt, or by building venture capital mitigating measures into the financing structure. This will limit the company's downside in case of unfavorable business conditions by allowing cash flow to be preserved as much as possible and allow a balancing upside in a successful business climate.

On the other hand, a company with low business risk can allow a higher financial gearing and use it to increase shareholder value. Thus, a large company that is strongly positioned in a growth market can thus improve the net present value of its investment strategies via debt financing, as long as the marginal price of capital remains below the internal rate of return.

These strategic considerations can be illustrated schematically as follows:

Business Risk	**Financial Risk**	
	Low	**High**
High	Overall risk reduced as low-risk financing structure supports high-risk business strategy	Overall risk level critically high
Low	Low use of financial gearing	Benefits from financial gearing

Figure 11.2 The combination of business and financial risk

Business risk is typically highest in start-up ventures and in the beginning of the product life cycle; in these situations a company should seek to reduce its financial risk. As business risk diminishes over time the financial risk can be altered, possibly through refinancing.
It must be noted that decision structures in family-owned businesses or closely held companies can differ from those described above. The owners may be reluctant to use high levels of financial gearing because of the increased risk and potential loss of independence and control.

Refinancing

As mentioned earlier, refinancing can be a strategic tool in the overall investment process. A key benefit of refinancing is that it can lower financing costs once a company has moved beyond the initial phases of its investment strategy and into a period of greater stability or continued growth. Here, its level of business risk decreases and refinancing may be justifed. The chart below illustrates how financial risk can be increased in line with reduced business risk:

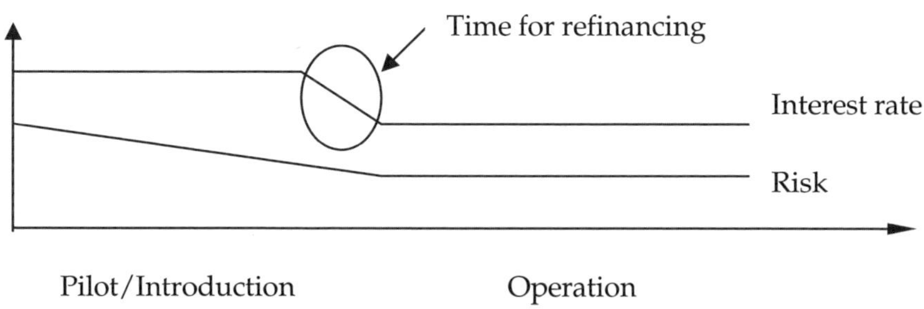

Figure 11.3 Time for refinancing

When a company exits the start-up phase and begins to operate as a going concern, the risks from adverse developments such as time schedule deviations and cost overruns tend to decrease in size. As they do, the company's marginal price of capital should diminish as well. When it does, it may be possible to replace expensive equity capital with debt financing. By this point not only has the business risk been reduced, but some of the initial debt financing will have been repaid and the equity/balance ratio will have gone up as a result. The investors may wish to bring the equity/balance ration back to its original level or even lower, now that the business risk is smaller. Refinancing is a tool that can help ensure a desired capital structure is maintained throughout the project period, or that it is changed in accordance with the company's changing risk profile.

CHAPTER 12

Uncertainty

Investments involve prediction, assumptions and judgment; and predictions about the future invariably involve uncertainty.

Predictions in the form of point estimates belie a fundamental lack of complete knowledge in regard to what the future will actually look like. The future is a range of possible outcomes, not a specific set of circumstances that will inevitably come to pass. A prediction about the future, as seen from the perspective of today, would have to describe every event that could happen and its associated probability. This can be thought of as a "possibility space" of all events and their associated likelihood at any point in time.

Consequently, there is a great deal of strategic uncertainty when considering the long run, which, naturally, investments are about. The longer the time horizon over which a strategy must play out, the greater the range of possible outcomes that must be considered. Yet, of course, the farther out we go, the less certain the probabilities associated with any result become.

The expectations about future cash flow that serve as the basis for financial calculations are informed estimates which contain a certain degree of uncertainty. They are almost never exact and certain figures. Ultimately, the degree of uncertainty depends on the specific project at hand.

For purely financial investments as we typically see in deposits, leasing, lending and the stock market, future cash flows are often specified in a loan document or other financial agreement. For example, we can estimate the expected future cash flow of deposits on a 3-6 month term account at a fixed interest rate with a relatively high degree of certainty. The same holds true, for instance, with cash flows for financial investments in short-term treasury bonds. The main uncertainties here will be related to the solvency and liquidity of the debtor. Financial investments in shares of stock, on the other hand, are fundamentally different. Their dividends and share prices have a higher degree of uncertainty and therefore require special evaluations and tools.

The uncertainty inherent in investments in real assets varies with each specific case. Investments in oil exploration and experimental drilling are typically associated with a high degree of uncertainty because the likelihood of finding commercial wells cannot be estimated with precision prior to a company's committing investment funds. On the other hand, a piece of real estate that will be rented to a solvent tenant on a long-term contract may be seen as a relatively certain investment.

We therefore need *methods for estimating and analyzing uncertainty which provide information that reduces investment risks.* The methods used can range from advanced mathematical and statistical models to much simpler calculations. The more advanced statistical methods find their use especially within the financial sector's realm, where they are used to evaluate risks related to financial investments. Meanwhile, the simpler methods are more used in investment decisions involving real assets.

A key point to understanding risks and uncertainties it to make good use of acquired experience and know-how within the specific area or industry being analyzed. Empirical data are valuable for understanding trends and developments, but they must be used with caution. A projection of historical data which lacks critical analysis can be very misleading, as would be the case if a Christmas tree salesman who, noting an increase in sales for three weeks in December, orders a large number of trees on 24 December.

The analysis of political, economic, sociologic, technological, environmental and legal developments for society or a particular industry, can provide important insights into how to reduce or respond to the uncertainty inherent in an investment decision.

In the following pages, we will describe four methods that can be used for evaluating the uncertainty and sensitivity of an investment project and the relevant data set. The four methods are:

1. Stochastic simulations.
2. Critical values.
3. Optimistic and pessimistic scenarios (i.e. worst and best-case scenarios).
4. Real options analysis - decision trees.

Stochastic Simulations

Stochastic simulation makes it possible to create an overview of the variation in a project's net present value when simulating variations in input data. Net present value is typically used as the outcome (or dependent) variable, but IRR can be used as well. Therefore, instead of assuming only one set of data for cash inflows and outflows, which is similar to a base case calculation, a stochastic simulation uses statistical distributions for the input factors, and then calculates a statistical distribution of the investment's expected net present value or internal rate of return. This is done by having a computer simulate potential investment outcomes many times to create a statistical distribution of the results. Each simulation is based on a new data set drawn from the statistical distributions. The computer simulation then generates an outcome of the project's expected NPV or IRR via a probability distribution, rather than a single number.

The simulation's results make it possible to obtain an impression of the project's most likely outcomes. At the same time it gives insight into the probability of getting a result above or below a certain pre-specified level.

Despite being very sophisticated and comprehensive, statistical simulation is somewhat difficult to use and typically requires a tailor-made computer program for each specific project. In addition, it is complicated to determine what statistical distributions should be used to properly describe the different factors included in the calculations. And finally, the results, since they are in the form of a comprehensive frequency distribution of NPVs and IRRs, can be quite overwhelming to interpret and use a basis for decisions.

Critical Values

Critical values provide a powerful tool for determining how much a given input value in the investment analysis can change before the investment becomes unattractive. We may calculate the critical value for any input variable, but in the large majority of cases, sales revenue is the most critical factor. When the critical value for sales volume is calculated, it is often referred to as a break-even analysis.

Critical values are often simpler to interpret and make decisions from than simulations. For instance, it is much easier for a sales representative to tell you if he considers his sales forecast to be relatively certain within a range of say ± 10 %, than it is for him to express the periodic standard deviation on the sales forecast.

To find critical values, we start by defining the minimum net present value we will accept for the project at hand. This will typically be 0, but it could be any other number we choose. Then we put the expected future cash flows in order and isolate the critical value for cash flow at each time "t", expressed as a function of the critical factor:

$$NPV_0 = \sum_{t=0}^{N} f(CF, critical\ factor)_t \cdot (1+I)^{-t} \ .$$

Then this equation is solved with regard to the critical factor.

It may be difficult or impossible to solve the equation directly, so we typically perform the calculations in a spreadsheet and use trial and error.

Example 12.1
A company is planning the construction of a new factory which will be used for the mass production of two different products. Management has

decided to use an investment horizon of ten years, and has set the minimum acceptable rate of return at 12 % per year. After some analysis, the production and sales staff is able to present management with the following table of financial information:

Year	Invest-ment	Units sold Prod 1	Units sold Prod 2	Cash flow Prod 1	Cash flow Prod 2	Net cash flow
0	€5,000,000					–€5,000,000
1	€1,500,000	600	400	€90,000	€80,000	–€1,330,000
2	€1,000,000	2,400	1,600	€360,000	€320,000	–€320,000
3	€1,000,000	4,200	2,800	€630,000	€560,000	€190,000
4		6,000	4,000	€900,000	€800,000	€1,700,000
5		7,500	5,000	€1,125,000	€1,000,000	€2,125,000
6		7,800	5,200	€1,170,000	€1,040,000	€2,210,000
7		8,100	5,400	€1,215,000	€1,080,000	€2,295,000
8		8,400	5,500	€1,260,000	€1,100,000	€2,360,000
9		8,500	5,500	€1,260,000	€1,100,000	€2,375,000
10		8,500	5,500	€1,275,000	€1,100,000	€2,375,000

The total investment of €8,500,000 is expected to be spread out over four years, with production to begin in the middle of the first year. An analysis of the market and industry indicates that the contribution margin per unit sold is stable over the forecast period and will likely follow the general price trends. Therefore, we will develop the investment analysis based on fixed prices and use a constant contribution margin per unit of €150 for Product 1 and €200 for Product 2. The marginal contributions have been fixed on the basis of sales prices of €275 and €350, and on direct average variable costs of €125 and €150, respectively. Given these assumptions, the project generates a net present value of €710,895 and an internal rate of return of 13.85 % per year. Using this analysis, the project is seen to be profitable. The question is, however, How much can the data deviate from these assumptions before the project becomes unprofitable?

If net cash flow in each year is divided into its separate components, the function for those cash flows can be written as:

$CF_t = -Inv_t + Quantity_{1,t} \cdot (Sales\ Price_1 - AVC_1\ ) + Quantity_{2,t} \cdot (Sales\ Price_2 - AVC_2)$

where:

Inv_t is the investment at Time t.
$Quantity_{1,t}$ is the expected sales in units of Product 1 at Time t.
$Quantity_{2,t}$ is the expected sales in units of Product 2 at Time t.

The net present value of the investment can be written as:

$$NPV_0 = \sum_{t=0}^{10} (-Inv_t + Quantity_{1,t} \cdot (Sales\ Price_1 - AVC_1) + Quantity_{2,t} \cdot (Sales\ price_2 - AVC_2)) \cdot (1+I)^{-t}.$$

The equation above may be rewritten:

$$NPV_0 = -Inv_t \cdot (1+I)^{-t} + \sum_{t=0}^{10} Quantity_{1,t} \cdot Sales\ Price_1 \cdot (1+I)^{-t} - \sum_{t=0}^{10} Quantity_{1,t} \cdot AVC_1 \cdot (1+I)^{-t} + \sum_{t=0}^{10} Quantity_{2,t} \cdot Sales\ Price_2 \cdot (1+I)^{-t} - \sum_{t=0}^{10} Quantity_{2,t} \cdot AVC_2 * (1+I)^{-t}.$$

If we want to calculate how much the sales volume of Product 2 must change in order for the net present value to reach a value of $NPV_{0,new}$, we would proceed as follows: First we replace "$quantity_{2,t}$" with the expression "$quantity_{2,t} \cdot (1 + X)$", where X represents only that percentage change in the sales forecast for Product 2 which yields the exact value of the net present value of $NPV_{0,new}$, which we have set as our hurdle rate.

Next, we replace the two following elements from the expression for NPV_0:

$$\sum_{t=0}^{10} \text{quantity}_{2,t} \cdot \text{Unit Price}_2 \cdot (1+I)^{-t} - \sum_{t=0}^{10} \text{quantity}_{2,t} \cdot \text{AVC}_2 \cdot (1+I)^{-t}$$

with:

$$\sum_{t=0}^{10} \text{quantity}_{2,t} \cdot (1+X) \cdot \text{Unit Price}_2 \cdot (1+I)^{-t} - \sum_{t=0}^{10} \text{quantity}_{2,t} \cdot (1+X) \cdot \text{AVC}_2 \cdot (1+I)^{-t},$$

which also may be written as:

$$\sum_{t=0}^{10} \text{quantity}_{2,t} \cdot \text{Unit Price}_2 \cdot (1+I)^{-t} - \sum_{t=0}^{10} \text{quantity}_{2,t} \cdot \text{AVC}_2 \cdot (1+I)^{-t}$$

$$+ X \cdot \sum_{t=0}^{10} \text{quantity}_{2,t} \cdot \text{Unit Price}_2 \cdot (1+I)^{-t} - X \cdot \sum_{t=0}^{10} \text{quantity}_{2,t} \cdot \text{AVC}_2 \cdot (1+I)^{-t}.$$

The first two sections in this new function are completely identical to Product 2´s initial contribution to the net present value. Therefore, the equation for the net present value which we have fixed as the hurdle value may be calculated as:

$$\text{NPV}_{0,new} = \text{NPV}_0 + X \cdot \sum_{t=0}^{10} \text{quantity}_{2,t} \cdot \text{Sales Price}_2 * (1+I)^{-t} - X \cdot \sum_{t=0}^{10} \text{quantity}_{2,t} \cdot \text{AVC}_2 \cdot (1+I)^{-t},$$

After a little rewriting, this yields:

$$\text{NPV}_{0,new} - \text{NPV}_0 = X \cdot \sum_{t=0}^{10} \text{quantity}_{2,t} \cdot \text{Contribution Margin}_2 \cdot (1+I)^{-t} \quad \text{or}$$

$$X = \frac{\text{NPV}_{0NEW} - \text{NPV}_0}{\sum_{i=o}^{10} \text{quantity}_{2,t} \cdot \text{Contribution Margin}_2 \cdot (1+I)^{-t}}.$$

This means that the percentage change in the sales forecast for Product 2 (which generates a specific net present value), may be determined as the change in net present value, divided by the present value of Product 2´s original contribution margin. This is true as long as the assumption that the contribution margin remains stable over the investment period is valid.

We can use this method to find the critical values at which the investment will turn unprofitable. That will happen when:

a) The actual values for price and sales volume differ from the forecast assumptions by more than:

	Product 1	Product 2
Price	8.50 %	10.00 %
Sales in units	15.63 %	17.72 %

b) The total sales of Products 1 and 2 drop more than 8.3 %.

These critical values enable the decision-makers to better consider project risk because they weigh the likelihood that actual business results will turn out differently from the estimates used for the investment analysis.

The calculation of critical values for a given investment can be performed with relative ease in a spreadsheet. It is done by setting the NPV value at a target number (most often NPV=0), then solving for each specific variable which the investor has defined as a critical value.

A drawback to critical values is that calculations are done under the assumption that all other factors in the investment are held constant. This may potentially underestimate the sensitivity of the investment project, as changes often happen simultaneously.

Worst and Best-case Scenarios

Scenario analysis is concerned with thinking through the possible future scenarios which an investment strategy may lead to, and it allows for simulating multiple concurrent changes in variables. In reality, deviations from an investment's assumptions are simultaneous. In the case of negative deviations, this may prove catastrophic for the project even though the new value for any single factor has not reached its critical value. Scenario building is the thing that makes this possible.

In the context of managing strategic uncertainty, scenarios are best thought of as specific descriptions of different futures. They are not ranges for specific variables such as interest rates, the price of oil, or the frequency occurrence of a natural or man-made disaster. Rather, scenarios provide an efficient way to summarize and synthesize the interaction of all relevant variables into a coherent picture. Different scenarios capture different, often extreme, values for the full set of relevant variables, as opposed to slight changes "at the margin" for individual variables.

In any scenario, there are likely to be a large number of relevant variables, too many to consider all at once. As a result, it is typically advisable to cluster these variables into specific dimensions of uncertainty. Therefore, as an example, interest rates, exchange rates, the price of oil, the general level of economic activity, and so forth might be variables which can reasonably be clustered together into a single dimension of uncertainty labelled as "the economy". The more dimensions of uncertainty one considers, the more detailed each scenario will be. However, the price of including greater detail is an exponentially more difficult analytical challenge when the scenarios are used as an input to strategic planning.

Determining the limits of uncertainty is a highly challenging task: Transcending preconceived notions and built-in limits which restrict the ability to imagine alternative futures is a delicate balancing act. It is more art than science, and the only way to develop the appropriate intuition is to review previous work and obtain a feel for what useful scenarios may look like.

Scenario analysis typically involves developing a worst and best-case scenario, starting from the investment's base case. The worst-case scenario is created by looking at the consequences which ensue when the investment's factors become sharply negative all at the same time. This could, for instance, happen when higher production costs are combined with downward pressure on prices and a reduction in sales volumes. Possible mitigating factors might also be taken into consideration, such as manufacturing efficiency gains which help improve overall cost performance in such a case. To sum up, the worst-case scenario should take into account the likely impact of negative developments in key factors to the project.

A best-case scenario will also typically be generated. Its purpose is to reflect the impact on net present value and IRR should the actual developments in key factors turn out to be more positive than the base case has assumed.

An investment project's decision makers can develop as many scenarios as they feel necessary, but usually at least three scenarios are created:

- A worst-case scenario.
- A base case scenario.
- A best-case scenario.

Example 12.2
Assume that an investment strategy shows a base case with a positive NPV of €710,895 and an IRR of 13.85 % p.a. The decision-makers would like to understand the risks and uncertainties underlying the project and have therefore asked for a worst-case and best-case scenario to be developed.

Compared to the base case scenario, the *worst-case scenario* has been defined to include:

- A cost overrun, where capital expenditures on fixed assets will be 5 % higher than budgeted.
- Sales volume of Product 1 will be 3 % lower.
- Sales volume of Product 2 will be 4 % lower.
- Marginal contribution for both products will be 2 % lower.

By simulating the financial consequences of these changes to assumptions in the base case, we see the project is not profitable. The net present value goes negative with a value of –€143,653, and the internal rate of return decreases to 11.63 % per year.

If we instead take an optimistic view, the *best-case scenario* will look like this:

- Capital expenditures on fixed assets are 3 % lower than budgeted.
- Sales of Product 1 are 3 % higher.
- Sales of Product 2 increase by 2 %.
- The marginal contribution for both products is 4 % higher.

This best-case scenario yields a net present value of €1,514,035 and a corresponding internal rate of return of 15.95 % per year.

In summary, we now have the following picture of the project's profitability:

Changes in assumptions:

	Fixed asset	**Sales P1**	**Sales P2**	**Contribution margin**	**NPV_0**	**Internal rate of return**
Worst Case	+5 %	–3 %	–4 %	–2 %	–€143,653	11.63 %
Base Case	0	0	0	0	€710,895	13.85 %
Best Case	–3 %	+3 %	+2 %	+4 %	€1,514,035	15.95 %

We see that even though the percentage changes in each of the factors are relatively modest, they lead to a change in net present value of more than 100 %.

Example 12.3
The Swedish pharmaceutical firm Medico recently developed a new drug which can be used for human and veterinary purposes. A similar product imported from the USA is already on the market in Sweden. However, Medico is convinced that its excellent relationships with general practitioners and veterinarians will enable it to take over almost the entire Swedish market if they can compete on price with the American company.

Today, the price of the American product is $7.50 per unit. In addition, expenses of $2.25 per unit must be added to cover freight and transportation costs, leading to a total price in Sweden of $9.75 per unit. It is expected that this price will remain fairly constant until new and better drugs are developed. If and when this happens, the current product would disappear from the market.

Current annual sales in the Swedish market are 325,000 units, and this number is expected to increase by 85,000 units per year over the coming years.

Based on market intelligence and business experience, Medico believes a new and better drug will not be ready to enter the market for another four to nine years. Most estimates expect the new product in approximately six years.

The raw materials used for production of the drug are supplied by a company based in Singapore. The purchase price for one finished product's worth of raw materials is SGD 2.50. The demand for these raw materials is expected to rise, leading to an cost increase of approximately 2 % per year in the following years.

A production plant for the new drug will cost SEK 130 million to construct. When this facility ceases operations, it will have a minimal scrap value which covers only the cost of dismantling it.

Maximum production capacity at the plant will be 1 million units per year. This is more than the total Swedish market can bear, but with increasing international brand recognition and high credibility, Medico expects to export its surplus production as long as it can continue competing on price with the American company. However, production is very sensitive because the chemical process is difficult to control. Moreover, governmental regulations are very strict so the approved annual production may either be larger or smaller than the company's 1 million units target.

At the time of the investment analysis, the exchange rate between SEK and US and Singapore dollars is SEK/USD 633 and SEK/SGD 380 DKK. Medico´s WACC before taxes is 12 % per year.

Based on the information at hand, we can construct the following table. The sales price for export markets is reduced by $2.25, which covers expenses in connection with freight and transport.

All amounts are in SEK

Year	1	2	3	4	5	6
Sales in units, Dom.	325,000	410,000	495,000	580,000	665,000	750,000
Retail price, SEK	61.72	61.72	61.72	61.72	61.72	61.72
Sales in units, export	675,000	590,000	505,000	420,000	335,000	250,000
Sales price, export	47.48	47.48	47.48	47.48	47.48	47.48
Raw material price	9.50	9.69	9.88	10.08	10.28	10.49
Contribution in mill.	42.6	43.6	44.6	45.7	46.7	47.7

Cash flow in million SEK

Year 0	Year 1	Year 2	Year 3	Year 4	Year 5	Year 6
–130.0	42.6	43.6	44.6	45.7	46.7	47.7

This yields a net present value of SEK 54.2 million and an internal rate of return of 24.1 % per year.

Although the project looks attractive, a number of uncertain factors call for further analysis:

1. For instance, the company expects its Swedish market sales to continue to grow. This demand is projected to increase by 85,000 units per year, or 25 % the first year. A less than expected increase in sales growth will naturally affect the investment's profitability. However, the impact is limited because the Swedish market would have to shrink dramatically for this to have a significant effect on the project. This is because the domestic market represents only 25 % of Medico's total production, and the difference in price between the Swedish market and the export market is only about 20 %. Consequently, a miscalculation in the growth rate of the Swedish market will have a very limited impact on the project's cash flow.
2. The sales price is largely determined by the American competitor, and Medico has very limited ability to set its own prices. A change in price will affect both its local and international markets. The export market is the more sensitive of the two, partly because approximately 75 % of Medico's production is intended for export, but also because this market's contribution margin is less than that in the Swedish market. If the global market price were to decline to less than $7.90 per unit, the project would become unprofitable. This corresponds to a decline in price of roughly 20 %.

The SEK-to-US dollar exchange rate is also subject to uncertainty, and the dollar has experienced a large decline of late. This adds a significant degree of risk to the investment and makes the American company's product cheaper on the international market. An exchange rate of 500 SEK/USD is the critical value which would make the project unprofitable.

The risk associated with fluctuations in the exchange rate between the SEK and the SGD is less critical, as only the raw materials are paid for in SGD.

The last risk element to consider is the pharmaceutical production itself. Production is complicated, and the chemical process is difficult to control. At the same time, the governmental requirements are very strict. Therefore, production volumes are likely to deviate from the budgeted figures. Simulations show that the project would become unprofitable if production volumes were to be 30 % lower than budgeted.

On this basis, we can develop Medico's worst-case and best-case scenarios. Below is a breakdown for each of the two scenarios:

	Base Case	**Worst Case**	**Best Case**	**Critical values**
Sales in units, year 1	325,000	325,000	325,000	
Increas in sales, units	85,000	60,000	100,000	
US$ exchange rate	633	550	650	480
SGD exchange rate	380	385	375	885
Sales price in US$	9.75	9.00	10.00	7.67
Raw material price in SGD	2.50	2.50	2.50	5.82
Increase in raw material price	2 % p.a.	3 % p.a.	1 % p.a.	39.78 % p.a.
Freight in US$	2.25	2.50	2.00	6.50
Production	1,000,000	900,000	1,100,000	648,729
IRR % p.a.	25.44	9.28	33.73	
Net present value, mill SEK	54.233	–9.999	90.821	

An additional risk factor concerns the possible entry of a better product into the market. One way to consider this risk is to analyze the payback.

Calculations show that the investment costs could be recovered over a period of four years if all other forecasts develop as anticipated.

As a final remark, it should be noted that a finance structure denominated in US dollars will reduce the project's risk because the company's exposure to fluctuations in the SEK/USD exchange rate will be more limited. A USD-denominated financing will make instalment payments (interest and principle) fluctuate at the same rate as sales revenue, thereby providing a hedge against this currency risk.

Real Options Analysis – Decision Trees

We have seen in Chapter 8 that using decision trees and real options provides an excellent starting point for developing and evaluating possible scenarios, as well as for managing an investment project's risks in a structured manner.

Real options are a powerful analytical tool which could be included in a company's investment project scenarios; they are also helpful in planning suitable strategic initiatives in support of these scenarios.

Based on the Medico example above, we can calculate an expected net present value if we assume that each of the three scenarios reviewed entails a certain probability.

Let us assume that the likelihood of the best-case scenario materializing is 10 %, that the base case is 50 %, and the worst-case 40 %. When we weight each scenario's net present value by its respective probability, we find that the investment strategy's total expected NPV is:

$NPV_0 = 10\ \% \cdot 90{,}821 + 50\ \% \cdot 54{,}233 + 40\ \% \cdot -9{,}999 = \text{SEK } 32.2 \text{ mill.}$

In order to make more informed decisions about a project and clarify uncertainties, investors will often conduct market research analysis and feasibility studies. We can analyze the cost benefit of an undertaking. Let us assume that a feasibility study will cost SEK 1 million and that, for simplicity, the study will result in one of two things: either Medico's underlying assumptions about initiating the project are "good", or they are "bad".

If the feasibility study concludes that the investment's outcome will be a good one, the probability of a best case, base case, and worst case is 60 %, 30 %, and 10 %, respectively.

On the other hand, if the feasibility study indicates that the company's assumptions are "bad", the chances of each scenario become 5 %, 5 %, and 90 %, respectively.

However, the results of the feasibility study are also uncertain. For the sake of simplicity, let us assume that there is a 50 % probability that the results are "good", and a 50 % probability that they are "bad".

Medico's hope, of course, is that the feasibility study will provide useful analysis and information. If it does, this will promote better decision-making which improves the likelihood that it will see a favorable outcome scenario .

Figure 12.1 shows we have the choice of initiating the investment without performing a feasibility study, or that we can conduct it and then, based on the results, decide whether to execute the project or not. Hence, the feasibility study provides additional information which may be helpful in the investment decision.

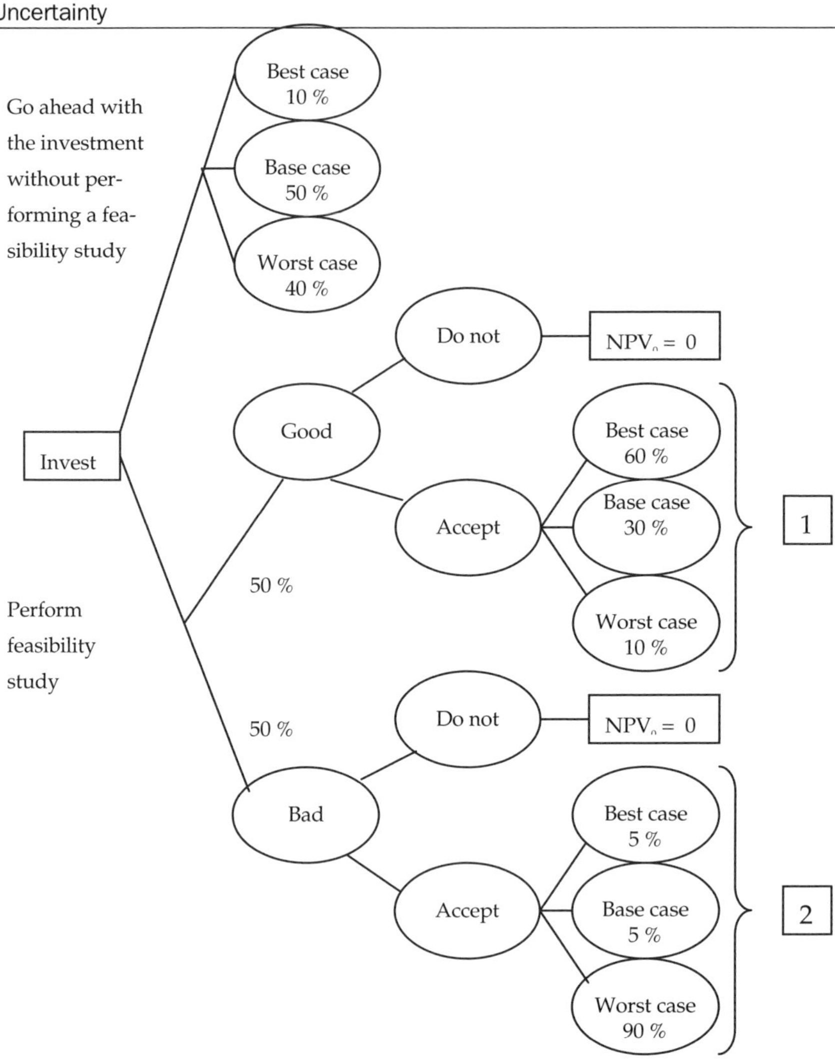

Figure 12.1 Decision tree for an investment, with or without a feasibility study

The decision process may be illustrated as follows:

1		2	
Best case:		Best case:	
90,821 · 60 %	= 54,493	90,821 · 5 %	= 4,541
Base case:		Base case:	
54,233 · 30 %	= 16,270	54,233 · 5 %	= 2,712
Worst case		Worst case	
–9,999 · 10 %	= –1,000	–9,999 · 90 %	= –9,000
Expexted NPV	= 69,763	Expexted NPV	= –1,747

If the conclusions of the feasibility study are that the background assumptions are "good", we see that the decision to initiate the project dominates the decision to not proceed. This is because the expected net present value from initiating the project is SEK 69.8 million, which is higher than the zero NPV from not initiating it. Naturally, we assume that a rational investor will choose to accept the project.

If, on the other hand, the results of the feasibility study show a "bad" outcome, the expected net present value will be negative, with a value of SEK -1.8 million. In this case we would expect the decision-maker to choose the dominating strategy of not initiating the investment, which again has an NPV of zero.

Now that we have used the feasibility study to determine which decisions are most rational, we can continue with a calculation about whether the study should be executed in the first place. From the decision tree, we observe that the expected net present value of the project without the feasibility study is SEK 32.2 million.

If we choose to carry out the feasibility study and afterwards make an "invest" or "not invest" decision based on its results, the expected net present value will be:

$NPV_0 = 50\ \% \cdot 69{,}763 + 50\ \% \cdot 0 - 1{,}000 =$ SEK 33.9 million.

Therefore, if we conduct a feasibility study and make our decision based on its conclusions, the expected net present value is modestly higher than if we made the investment without one. In this case, then, the study is advantageous.

An important added benefit of conducting the feasibility study is that it improves the investment strategy's risk profile because the probability of a worst-case scenario decreases from 40 % to 10 %. Thus, uncertainty is reduced if the study is performed.

Another primary advantage of using the decision tree approach is that a company's investors are "forced" to make their strategic alternatives explicit. As they do, the value of the information they gather is included directly included in the investment calculations.

So, this method explicitly defines the investment's uncertainty, as well as the strategic decision alternatives which a company's management must face.

EXERCISES

Exercise 1

An investment is expected to generate the following net cash flows:

Year	0	1	2	3	4	5
Net Cash Flow	–100	40	30	30	20	20

A. *What is the net present value of the investment if a discount rate of 10 % and 20 % per year, respectively, are used?*

The investment will experience straight-line depreciation over 5 years. The tax rate is 30 %.

B. *What is the net present value of the project after taxes?*

Exercise 2

A company plans to purchase a specialized forklift truck at a price of €200,000. Doing so will lead to labor savings of €78,000 per year, all-inclusive. On the other hand, it will cost the company €28,000 per year to operate the truck (including gas, oil changes, maintenance, etc.). After 5 years, the scrap value of the truck will be €15,000.

A. *What is the internal rate of return for this investment?*
B. *Does the investment satisfy the company's requirement of a return of 8 % per year?*
C. *What will the average yearly savings and costs be if the company purchases the truck?*

Exercise 3

A company plans to invest in a new type of technology. Expectations are that a certain technology can generate savings of €27,460 per year for the next 8 years. The company utilizes a WACC of 7 % per year.

A. *What is the highest price that the company would be willing to pay for the new technology?*

Exercise 4

At its upcoming board meeting, the management of Bellafoss will discuss the best way to enter a promising new health food market. There are two possibilities it will consider:

A. Build its own production facility.
B. Buy an existing manufacturer on the market.

Alternative A:
Building a new production facility is projected to cost €5 million. Bellafoss expects first year revenues to cover expenses, but does not anticipate a profit. In the second year, positive cash flow (contribution margin) should be €2 million, increasing by an additional €2 million in each of the following two years. The company plans to spend €1 million on advertising during the first year and €500,000 for each of the next three years. The company has chosen to analyze the investment over a 4-year period because what the market will look like beyond this point is anybody's guess.

Alternative B:
The other possibility is for Bellafoss to acquire an existing manufacturer which already has a market position. Management believes that buying an existing company will result in a faster market entry. This would lead to a contribution margin (positive cash flow) of €1.2 million in the first year. During all of the following years the contribution margin is expected to be 20 % higher than the level estimated in Alternative A, i.e. € 2.4 million in Year 2. However, taking over the other company will involve post-acquisition costs in connection with administration and coor-

dination. These extra costs will amount to a total an anticipated €400,000 per year over the next 4 years. The advertising budget will be the same as Alternative A in all four years. Bellafoss operates with a discount rate of 12 % per year.

A. *What is the maximum price Bellafoss should pay to acquire the existing company?*

Exercise 5

A company has the choice between two alternative methods for producing its manufactured goods. The equipment used in Method 1 costs €5 million and has a lifetime of 10 years, whereas the type of equipment used in Method 2 costs €10 million but has a lifetime of 15 years. It is assumed that identical replacements are available for both types of equipment. Production vary directly with the production output and are €500 per produced unit for Method 1 and €400 per produced unit for Method 2. The company operates with a discount rate of 12 % per year.

A. *Calculate the production output where the two methods have equal production costs per unit.*

Exercise 6

You are faced with two investment projects, X and Y. Both investments require an initial outlay of €10,000 and will see the respective cash flows show in the table below. The discount rate is 12 % per year.

Year	Project X	Project Y
0	–10,000	–10,000
1	6,500	3,500
2	3,000	3,500
3	3,000	3,500
4	1,000	3,500

A. *Calculate the net present value, the internal rate of return, and the payback period for each project.*
B. *If the two investments are independent, which investment should be selected?*
C. *If the two investments are mutually exclusive, which one should be picked?*
D. *Does the discount rate affect the profitability ranking of the two investments?*
E. *Do you see a paradox in using the net present value to rank the investments' profitability on the one hand, versus using the internal rate of return on the other? If so, explain why this exists.*

Exercise 7

A farmer is thinking about investing in a windmill in order to cover her electricity needs. She has received a €21,000 quote for a windmill with 22 kWh of generating capacity. Operating and maintaining the windmill is covered by the supplier at a fixed cost of €210 per year. The expected lifetime of the windmill is 15 years. The farmer's revenue for this potential investment consists of the savings on her electricity bill. Accounting for weather conditions, the windmill should be able to provide 34,100 kWh of power per year. The price per kWh supplied by the general power company is €0.075 (including state charges). Because the windmill is expected to produce more electricity than the farmer can use, only 80 % of the electricity generated will be utilized; the remaining 20 % will be lost. Assume that all prices are fixed, that the real interest rate is 5 % per year, and that fiscal conditions are ignored.

A. *Calculate the investment's net present value and internal rate of return. Is the investment profitable?*

The supplier has suggested that the windmill could be re-engineered so that the farmer's remaining 20 % of production could also be utilized. Another possibility also exists: The windmill could be connected to the power distribution network so that the excess electricity produced could be delivered to the normal power supply. This would require an additional investment of €1,500 Electricity supplied to the power distribution network will yield €0.032 per kWh. The lifetime of this additional investment is expected to be 25 years.

B. *Is the additional investment profitable?*

As a final alternative, the windmill can be connected to the farmer's oil-fired burner so that any excess electricity could be used to provide hot water. The additional investment is expected to cost €3,000, and should generate savings of 0.2 liters of heating oil per kWh. The price of heating oil is €0.26 per liter, and the lifetime of the additional investment is estimated at 25 years.

C. *Is the additional investment profitable?*

The farmer believes that the profitability of the windmill project will depend on the future price of electricity. Therefore, she is interested in a sensitivity analysis, where she wishes to consider the investment in the windmill supplemented by the best of the three alternatives. It is assumed that the price of delivering electricity to and from the power distribution network will change at the same percentage rate as the price of heating oil,

D. *By how much will energy prices have to change in order to make the investment profitable or unprofitable?*

Exercise 8

An airline company is faced with having to replace its entire fleet of aging airplance. In deciding upon a new fleet, the airline can choose between two types of aircraft. Type 1 is a traditional airliner, and Type 2 is a newly developed aircraft which consumes less fuel and requires less maintenance. The data for the each type of aircraft are listed below:

	TYPE 1	TYPE 2
Cost of aircraft	€12 million	€16 million
Annual energy consumption	€2.5 million	€2.25 million
Other annual operating costs	€1.8 million	€1.64 million
Expected scrap value	€2.0 million	€2.4 million

The operating costs have been calculated based on assumptions about the use of the planes as measured in kilometers flown. This is because both the energy consumption and other operating costs are assumed to be proportional to the amount of kilometers flown. The company uses a discount rate of 9 % per year and all prices are fixed for purposes of this analysis. Tax considerations are ignored.

A. *Which type of aircraft should the company choose if each has a useful life of 15 years?*
B. *After reviewing the new airplane design's advances, the airline believes the new plane's useful life will be 20 years instead of 15. Does this adjustment impact the purchase decision if the existing design's useful life remains unchanged?*

The operating costs have been calculated based on the assumption that the cost of fuel will not change in the future. Management believes the cost will be more volatile than many expect, so it would like to know how sensitive the investment calculation is to changes in the cost of fuel.

C. *If the useful lives of the airplanes remain at 15 years for the existing design and 20 years for the new style, how much would the fuel price have to change for the two aircraft types to be cost the same amount of money? Assume the planes' useful lives are the same as those described in Question B.*

Exercise 9

A company is considering whether or not to start producing a new product. A number of analyses have been performed in order to clarify the demand for the product and detail the production costs. The results of these analyses are given below:

- Acquisition of production equipment: €1,000,000.
- The machinery is depreciated per the declining-balance method at a fixed percentage rate of 30 %, which corresponds to the actual loss of market value.
- The cost of maintaining the equipment is expected to be €50,000 the first year and increasingg by 20 % per year thereafter.
- In order to start marketing the new product the company must spend €400,000 on an advertising campaign during the first year. In the following years the company expects to spend €100,000 on its marketing costs.
- The machinery has a production capacity of 9,000 units per year, with variable costs of €210 per unit.
- In order to operate the machinery, the company must hire 10 employees, each with a salary of €36,000 per year.
- The product can be sold on the market for €300 per unit.
- The company has a discount rate of 10 % per year.

A. *If the company has a 5-year time horizon and believes it can sell the equipment at any time for its depreciated (market) value, should it make the decision to purchase?*

B. *What is the optimal time frame for replacing the equipment with new, identical equipment?*

Exercise 10

In order to manufacture one of its new products, a company has acquired a production facility for €3.5 million. The facility's value depreciates 10 % per year using straight-line depreciation. The operating costs, which include product research and development will be €1 million in Year 1 and increase at 25 % per year thereafter. The product generates a contribution margin of €300,000 per month and the company uses a discount rate of 15 % per year. Tax and inflation issues are ignored.

A. *How long should the company continue manufacturing the product?*

Exercise 11

Three years ago a company purchased a production facility for €1,000,000 in cash. The facility is depreciated with a fixed percentage of 30 % per year, which corresponds to the actual decline in value. Its operating and maintenance costs were €45,000 in the first year and have increased by €45,000 per year in Years 2 and 3. This rate of increase is expected to be constant in the years to come. In order to smooth out fluctuations in its available cash on hand, the company has a revolving line of credit with its bank whose interest rate is 15 % per year. The production facility is used to manufacture a large portion of the company's product line and achieves an, annual contribution margin of €450,000. This contribution margin is expected to remain constant in the future.

A. *If the company wishes to close this production, when is the optimal time to do so?*
B. *If the company would like to continue production, when should it replace this facility with a similar one?*
C. *Assume that today, the company has the choice of acquiring a production facility with the same characteristics as the one described above. What is the maximum price it should pay for the new facility if the product's lifetime is 5 years and the equipment can be sold at this point for its scrap value?*
D. *How large should the annual contribution margin be if the company expects to pay exactly €1,000,000 for the replacement facility?*

Exercise 12

A new printing machine at Digiprint takes one year and €10 million to develop. Moreover, it costs €3 million in the first year to market the new machine. Afterwards, the marketing costs will be €2 million per year over the remaining life of the product. Digiprint expects to sell the printing machine for €700 per unit. The variable costs, including maintenance of the production machinery, are estimated to €450 per unit. The industry's product life cycle is typically characterized by 3 years during which the company can charge full price for the product, then 2 years where it can charge half price. Digiprint's cost of capital is 15 % per year and it ignores tax and inflation considerations for purposes of this analysis.

A. *How many printing machines must the company sell each year for the investment in development costs to be profitable?*

Digiprint is also evaluating the possibility of reducing its price well below the competition's, to €600 per unit. At the same time, it believes it can reduce its annual marketing expenses to one-third of the current level.

B. *Given the above changes in sales price and marketing expenses, how many printing machines must the company sell now in order for the investment to be profitable?*

Exercise 13

At an international fair for machine tools, the head of Global Tools, Ltd. establishes contact with a certain German manufacturer in attendance. The manufacturer offers to build a production facility which can produce a specialized tool in less time than it takes Global Tools to produce the tool at its existing plant. This will make it possible to reduce the cycle time per unit to 30 minutes on all three shifts, which corresponds to a per-shift increase of 1,600 units per quarter. With this new production facility, Global Tools will realize additional quarterly profits of €500,000. It will use 25 % per year straight-line depreciation and be sold for book value at the end of the third year of operations. The company has a 40 % tax-rate and will pay its tax at the end of the following year. It uses a nominal discount rate of 25 % per year before taxes and calculates interest quarterly.

A. *How much profit will the company make per quarter if the new production facility is implemented over the next three years?*
B. *If the company is to be profitable over a three-year time period, what is the maximum price that the company should pay for the new production facility?*

Exercise 14

Hansen & Co., Inc. produces a variety of plastic blanks for use in the automotive industry. The company has a number of fully automatic injection molding machines which run a combined 21,120 machine-hours per year. The machines are used exclusively in the production of Hansen & Co.'s two products, "Single" and "Multiple". The company is contemplating whether or not to begin manufacturing a third product, "Future", which would require a capacity expansion. The company normally offers its customers 30-day credit terms on purchased products. On the supplier side, it must pay for half of its raw materials in cash and receives 60-day credit terms on the remaining half. The raw materials inventory averages two months in stock before being used in production and there is no finished goods warehouse.

In order to decide whether or not the production facility should be expanded, the sales and production departments have gathered the following information about the three products, which have independent sales:

	Single	**Multiple**	**Future**
Sales in units per year	40,000	30,000	60,000
Price per unit	€200	€300	€170
Raw material unit cost	€170	€240	€110
Machine time in minutes	6 minutes	30 minutes	15 minutes

An additional injection molding machine has a capacity of 5,280 machine-hours per year. The machine would cost €1,750,000 including installation, setup, and debugging. After 4 years the facility will be obsolete and its scrap value will only cover the dismantling costs. Hansen & Co. uses a discount rate of 10 % per year.

A. *Should the expand its production capacity and if so, by how many facilities?*

Exercise 15

Multigoods, Inc. is both a cocoa processing and trading company. The manager of the company has just received a suggestion from one of the employees regarding a new product, which Multigoods Inc. could process on its own. The idea sounds promising. Market research indicates that the company could sell 5,000 tons of the new product in Year 1 at a price of €150 per ton and increase this quantity to 7,000 tons in Year 2 and following. Operating costs are estimated at €100 per ton

Manufacturing the new product requires investing in a specialized grinding machine which costs €800,000. Of this, €400,000 must be paid upon receiving the machine and €200,000 in each of the two years following. The grinding machine has an estimated lifetime of 5 years, after which point it must be scrapped as completely worthless. Multigoods uses straight-line depreciation over the machine's expected lifetime and incorporate of a discount rate of 12 % per year.

A. *At the next board meeting, should the manager recommend that the company begin production of this new processed cocoa product.*
B. *What the sales price per ton be set at if the investment to be profitable?*

Exercise 16

Perfect-Sound is thinking of producing an exclusive integrated sound system. The company has analyzed its competitors and the market and concluded that the retail price should be set at €8,100. The cost of raw materials is assumed to be €3,500 per unit, with labor at €2,500 per unit.
The sales department created a two-year sales forecast and determined that quarterly sales for the first, second, and third quarters of Year 1 will be 7, 27, and 37 units, respectively. From that point on, sales will be 40 units per quarter until the end of Year 2. After this point, however, the uncertainty becomes too great to create a forecast because the technology advances at a very rapid rate. Raw materials and wage costs are paid in cash, and Perfect-Sound extends 60-days credit terms to its customers.

A. *Please establish a cash budget showing the changes in liquidity on a quarterly basis once production begins.*

To bring this new sound system to market, Perfect-Sound believes it will need to invest another €100,000 beyond the €250,000 it has already spent on research and development. The project is financed using a bank overdraft with no commission. However, the interest rate is 12 % per year with interest calculated on a quarterly basis.

B. *Should Perfect-Sound stop the new project immediately or plan to start production?*

Exercise 17

Currently, a new concrete production facility with advanced technology is being established in the vicinity of Sand Mountain's gravel pit. The concrete company has asked to receive a bid on 2,000 loads of gravel per year, with a special grain-size characteristic. It has agreed to pay a fixed price for a set amount of loads over a certain number of years and will arrange pickup with its own fleet of trucks. Sand Mountain produces gravel using specialized equipment, which has an initial purchase price of €1,000,000. With production of 2,000 loads per year, the annual costs for Year 1 amount to:

Wages:	€180,000
Maintenance	€90,000
Electricity	€50,000
Expected annual costs	€320,000

The machinery has a high content of very expensive parts and therefore loses its market value quickly. In fact, by the end of the first year of operations its scrap value will be zero. Nonetheless, it can continue to produce gravel for many years as long as it is maintained. The maintenance costs increase by 40 % each year, until they plateua at €500,000 per year. Once this level has been reached, they are expected to remain constant. The owner of the gravel pit would like to have an annual profit of €200,000 (exclusive of general and administrative costs, which are ignored), and he has set the company's WACC at 8 % per year.

A. *Given the above circumstances, what is the minimum retail price the gravel can be sold for. What operation and sales lifetime is assumed in connection with this price?*
B. *If the gravel is sold at this price, what are the financial consequences if the lifetime is increased or decreased by one year, respectively?*

Exercise 18

In order to align itself with industry advances, Yachting Inc. has asked a manufacturing consultant to examine the technological aspects of its production process. It feels that its equipment is quickly becoming obsolete and feels it will not survive if it does not invest in new technology in order to increase its yacht-building efficiency. Per the consultant's recommendation, the company has investigated two new assembly lines and received the following data:

Assembly line A:
The initial cost is €6 million and has a projected useful life is 7 years, after which point the it can be sold for a scrap value €300,000. The annual cost savings from manufacturing efficiency gains results from the decrease in the number of employees required in the production process. This labor savings is estimated at €2,000,000 per year. The assembly line's mainte-

nance costs are expected to be €200,000 in the first year and by €10,000 per year thereafter for the remaining life of the machine.

Assembly line B:

The initial cost is €5 million and the assembly line has a 4-year lifetime and no scrap value. It is depreciated at a straight-line rate over this lifetime. Maintenance costs are estimated at €300,000 in the first year and will increase by 10 % per year in the following years. The cost savings from efficiency gains will equate to €2,500,000 per year. The company utilizes a discount rate of 11 % per year.

A. *Assuming that one of the two alternatives should be chosen and that Yachting, Inc. will replace its assembly line with identical equipment in the future, which alternative should it invest in?*

Exercise 20

A company plans to invest €2,500,000 in a new machine. It is considering a number of financing opportunities and has a cost of capital of 10 % per year.:

- Cash purchase.
- Downpayment €1,000,000, with the supplier financing the balance. Two payments of €900,000 each must be made one and two years from now.
- Raising a 5-year 6 % bond at a price of €98 with equal annual installment payments. After financial costs of €8,800 have been deducted, the net proceeds must cover the cost of the machine.

A. *Which of the three financing options should the company choose?*

Exercise 21

A loan of €100,000 must be repaid over a 5-year with equal quarterly repayments of principal and interest. The interest rate is 2 % per quarter.

A. *What will the quarterly repayments and interest be?*
B. *What is the loan's effective interest rate?*

The bank has offered to structure the loan as a bond with a price of 95.

C. *What are the answers to Questions A and B, given the new information?*

The term of the loan is now changed to 10 years instead of 5 years. The price is still 95.

D. *What are the answers to Questions A and B now?*

Exercise 22

One of a company's key vendors is offering revised credit terms as follows:

- Cash payments within 5 days – minus 1.5 %.
- Current month plus 20 days – net cash.

A. *Calculate the effective interest rate for the vendor's credit.*

Exercise 23

A company has received three loan offers from various banks to finance a capital expenditure. In each case, the principal of €1,000,000 is enough to cover the investment and the financial costs of the three loans can be ignored. The loans are structured as follows:

- A 5-year bond with a nominal interest rate of 7 % per year and semi-annual payments of principal and interest. This bond can be raised at an offered price of 95.95.
- A 5-year bond with equal annual payments at a nominal interest rate of 8 % per year. This bond can be raised at a price of 99.50.
- A 5-year bond with quarterly payments and a nominal interest rate of 7.5 % per yea,. The effective interest rate on this loan is 2 % per quarter.

A. *Establish the cash flows from net proceeds and the payment cash flows pertaining to each bond. Also, calculate the bond price for the third financing offer.*

B. *Calculate the effective interest rate per year for each of the three loans (tax considerations may be ignored).*

C. *Which of the three financing offers should the company choose?*

We will now assume the following with regard to the company's tax conditions:

- As a borrower, the company can deduct interest payments and receive an immediate tax saving of 34 % of the interest paid.
- The company can immediately deduct a capital loss at the time when the bonds are raised.

D. *Given the above-mentioned tax conditions, develop a table (preferably in Excel), which illustrates the repayments and interest on an after-tax basis for each of the first two loans.*

E. *Which of these two loans should the company choose based on after-tax considerations?*

Exercise 24

A company has been offered two alternative loans which will be used to finance an expansion of its production capacity.

Alternative A: A fixed loan with a term horizon of 5 years. Loan raised in SEK.

Principal:	SEK 6,000,000
Quotation price:	96
Interest:	6 % per year with quarterly interest payments, due on a continuous basis over the life of the loan
Loan application handling fee:	0.1 % of principal
Commission:	0.4 % of principal
Stamp duty:	1.5 % of principal

Alternative B: A fixed loan with a term horizon of 5 years. Loan raised in SGD.

Principal:	1,500,000 SGD (daily exchange rate of 3.86 SEK)
Repayment:	500,000 SGD after the second year 500,000 SGD after the fourth year 500,000 SGD after the fifth year
Loan application handling fee and stamp duty:	1 % of the principal
Annual pre-paid underwriting commission:	2 % of the remaining debt
Annual Interest:	3 % pre-paid

A. *What is the effective interest rate for each of the two alternatives?*

Exercise 25

A company's steel fabrication department is faced with having to replace one of its drill presses. It has received offers from 3 different suppliers, each of whom is willing to supply a similar machine.

- The first offer is for €100,000 cash on delivery.
- The second offer is €110,000 with a 5 % annual yield, repaid over a 5-year period with equal fixed annual instalments.
- The third offer is a leasing contract, where the company can lease the machine for 5 years at a price of €26,000 per year.

After 5 years, the drill press will need to be replaced and have zero scrap value. When evaluating investments, the company uses a discount rate of 7 % per year.

A. *Which of the three offers should the company accept?*
B. *Are there any factors which might cause the company to decline the most advantageous offer?*

Exercise 26

Jane & John Smith own a clothing company named J&J Fashion. They have decided to expand their shopping mall location and expect to incur a cost of approximately €10 million in connection with this. They have two alternative financing offers:

Alternative A:
A 3-year bullet loan raised in USD:

Principal:	USD 12,500,000
Daily exchane rate:	1.25 USD/EUR
Annual fixed prepaid interest:	4 % per year of the remaining debt

It is assumed that the exchange rate of USD to the EUR will increase at a 2 % annual rate over the next 3 years. Furthermore, it is assumed that there are no additional costs associated with raising a loan in a foreign currency.

Alternative B:
A 3-year bond with equal payments of principal and interest in quarterly installments according to the following terms:

Principal:	€10,000,000
Loan application handling fee:	1 % of the principal
Commitment commission:	0.5 % of the principal
Stamp duty:	1.5 % of the principal
Bond price:	98
Nominal interest rate:	5 % per year, paid at a quarterly rate of 1.25 %

A. *Which of the two loan alternatives would you recommend that J&J Fashion pursue?*
B. *State which factors cause you to select this alternative as the most rational financing decision.*

Exercise 27

Despite its sizeable stockholders equity, Medivinci still faces large capital requirements if it wishes to continue developing its products and reputation with its target markets. The company wishes to maintain a high current ratio in order to exploit strategic opportunities and refinance its current loans. Medivinci has been offered an irredeemable 3-year bond loan in the international capital market by an established merchant bank in London. The proposed loan terms are as follows:

- Nominal principal on the loan: 3 million USD (exchange rate 1.25 USD/EUR).
- Repayment: 1/3 (33.33 %) of the principal by the end of each year.
- Total borrowing costs: 1 % of the principal.

- Fixed prepaid interest covering the entire term of the loan: 5 % per year of the remaining debt.
- Medivinci and its bank expect that the exchange rate of USD/EUR will increase at a rate of 1 % per year.

A. *What is the effective rate of interest per year in EUR if Medivinci raises the loan?*

B. *State the factors Medivinci must keep in mind if it chooses to raise the loan.*

Exercise 28

A company has performed a number of calculations and sensitivity analyses on an investment project it plans to undertake. However, before making a final decision, the company may decide to perform a market analysis.

A. *Sketch what the decision process might look like in a decision tree.*

Exercise 29

A company wishes to expand its chocolate sales on the Canadian market and establish itself as a solid participant. In order to do so, it needs to consider its options and weigh them from a strategic point of view.

A. *Sketch the considerations you think the company should include before making a final decision.*

B. *Create a decision tree for this project with relevant scenarios and development sequences which you find important.*

LITERATURE

Anderson, Torben Juul: *Real options analysis in strategic decision making: an applied approach in a dual options framework.* Journal of applied management studies, Vol 9. No 2, 2000.

Botteron, Pascal and Casanova, Jean-Francois: *Start-ups defined as portfolios of embedded options.* Research Paper no. 85, May 2003, FAME, Geneva.

Bodie, Zvi and Merton, Robert C.: *Finance.* Prentice Hall, Upper Saddle River, New Jersey. 1997

Brach, Marion A: *Real options in practice.* John Wiley & Sons, 2003.

Buckley, Adrian: *International Investments.* Copenhagen Business School Press, 1998

Christensen, Peter Ove og Sørensen, Bjarne Graabech: *Investeringsteori.* Odense Universitetsforlag, 2005

Christensen, Peter Ove og Sørensen, Bjarne Graabech: *Rentesregning.* Odense Universitetsforlag, 1994

Cissell, Robert, Cissell, Helen and Flaspohler, David C.: *Mathematics of Finance.* Eighth Edition. Houghton Mifflin Company. Boston, 1990

Contractor, Farok J and Lorange, Peter: *Cooperative Strategies and Alliances.* Pergamon, 2002.

Copeland, Tom and Tufano, Peter: *A real-world way to manage real options.* Harvard Business Review, March 2004.

Estrin, Saul & Meyer, Klaus E: *Investment Strategies in Emerging Markets.* Edward Elgar, 2004.

Fabrycky, W.J, Thuesen, G.J. and Verma, D.: *Economic Decision Analysis.* Third Edition. Prentice Hall, Upper Saddle River, New Jersey. 1998

Hirst, I.R.C.: *Business Investment Decisions.* Philip Allan, 1988

Jensen, Bjarne Astrup: *Rentesregning.* Jurist- og Økonomforbundets Forlag. 1996

Kim, W. Chan and Mauborgne, Renée: *Blue Ocean Strategy.* Harvard Business School Press, 2005

Levy, Hain and Sarnat, Marshall: *Capital Investment and Financial Decisions._Fifth Edition.* Prentice Hall International UUK) Ltd, 1994

Luehrmann, Timothy A: *Strategy as a Portfolio of Real Options.* Harvard Business Review, September-October 1998.

Lynggaard, Peter: *Investeringskalkuler.* Handelshøjskolens Forlag, 2003

Lynggaard, Peter: *Investering og finansiering.* Handelshøjskolens Forlag, 2003 (1987)

Myers, Stewart C and Brealey, Richard A: *Principles of corporate finance.* McGraw-Hill/Irwin, 2003.

Pedersen, Frank: *Investeringsplanlægning,* 7. rev. udgave. Systime A/S, 1995

Raynor, Michael E: *The Strategy Paradox.* Doubleday, 2007

Ross, Stephen A., Westerfield, Randolph W. and Jordan, Bradford D.: *Fundamentals of Corporate Finance. Fifth Edition.* Irwin McGraw-Hill, 2000

Salvatore, Dominick: *Managerial Economics in a Global Economy.* Oxford University Press, 2007 (1993)

Shapiro, Alan C: *Capital budgeting and investment analysis.* Pearson Prentice Hall, 2004.

Thomson, John and Martin, Frank: *Strategic Management.* Thomson, 2005

Trigeorgis, Lenos: *Real options and business strategy.* Risk Books, 1999.

Trigeorgis, Lenos: *Real options in capital investment.* Praeger, 1996.

Wigandt, Bruno: *Finansiel planlægning og investering.* Merko. Gyldendal Undervisning, 1997 (1989)